CCTV

快乐中国——学汉语

Happy China — Learning Chinese

中国中央电视台
《快乐中国——学汉语》栏目组 编

新疆篇

下

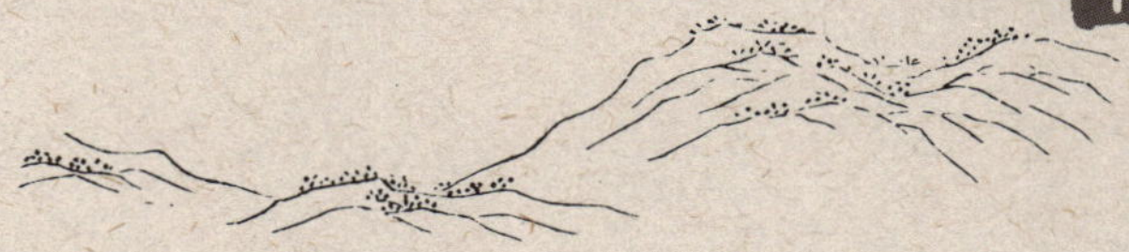

北京语言大学出版社

新疆主要景点游览示意图

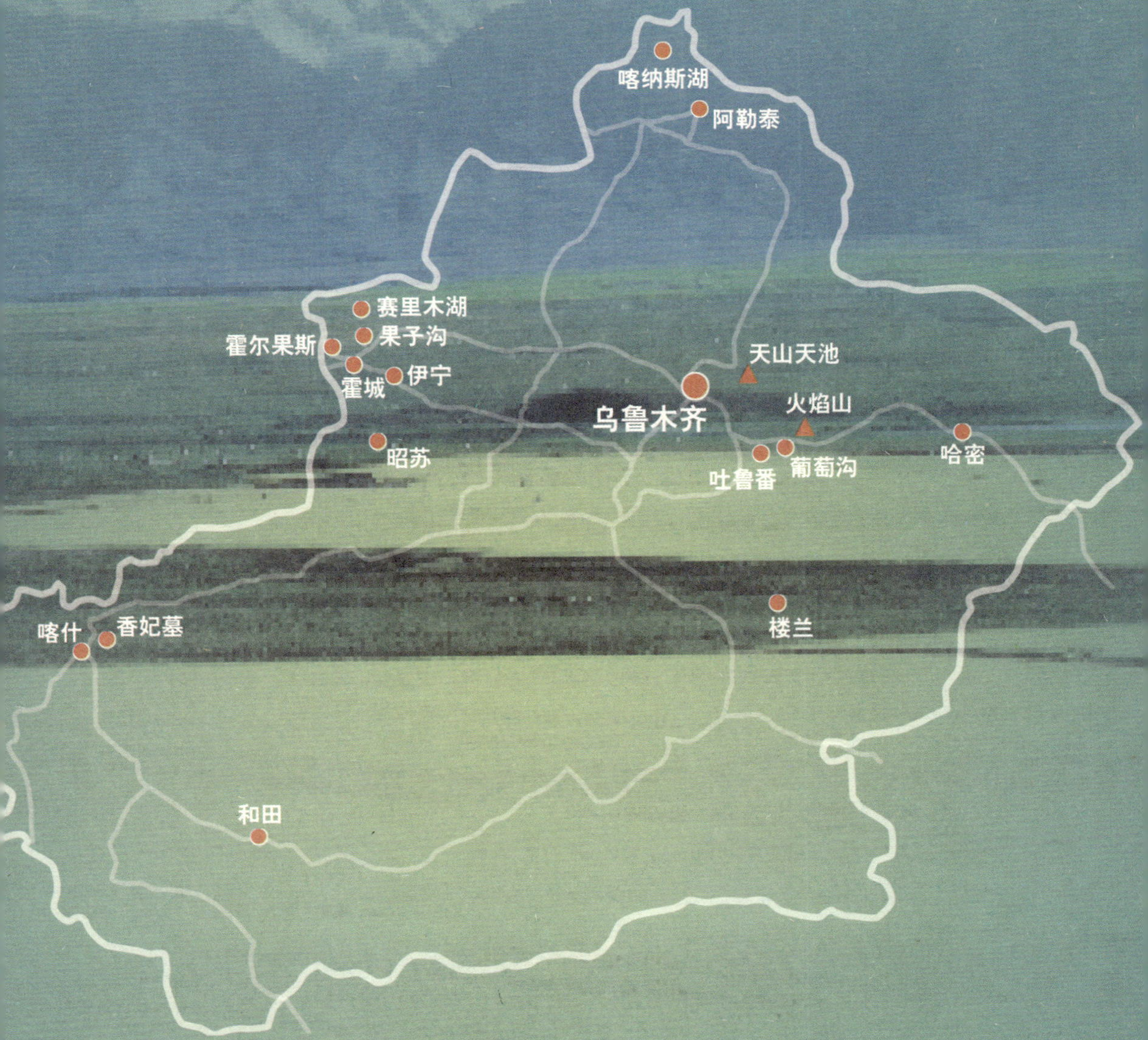

前　言

中国的发展令世人瞩目，随之而来的学汉语热潮也在全球兴起。

中国中央电视台中文国际频道（CCTV-4）《快乐中国——学汉语》栏目，与中国各地城市以及风景名胜点合作，把饱览名山大川、感受中华民族历史文化与学习汉语结合起来，将汉语言语技能与知识性、趣味性和欣赏性融为一体，创办了独特的寓教于乐的电视教学节目——《快乐中国——学汉语》。

通过中央电视台覆盖全球98%的强势传媒，《快乐中国——学汉语》自2004年6月播出以来，引起了海内外观众的热烈反响。不少观众来信来电，希望得到《快乐中国——学汉语》栏目播出节目的文字和音像材料，作为学习汉语的视听说教材。为了满足广大观众的需要，北京语言大学出版社承担了这套文字、声像教材的编辑、出版任务。在此，我们深表感谢！

语言是桥梁，电视是桥梁，《快乐中国——学汉语》是沟通你我的桥梁。它把汉语教学搬进大自然的课堂之中，“快乐学汉语，轻松又好记！”此外，我们采用高清晰电视技术和立体声制作的表现手段，并制作成可用于教学的、有多种字幕选择的DVD，充分展示汉语特有的魅力。

为了使节目主持人的对话更好地帮助您学说汉语，我们聘请了北京语言大学长期从事对外汉语教学和英语教学的几位教授，对每一集对话进行了加工，增添了生词、注释、替换练习和会话等部分，并负责生词和注释部分的英文翻译。每一集有8～10个生词，有5～8个注释，有模仿练习，也有交际性的活用练习，帮助您更好地理解对话内容，掌握重点词句。

为了适应学习者需要，每册收入15集节目（特殊情况除外），并配有相应拍摄点的简介、图片和旅游资讯。由于节目制作还在进行之中，配套图书将陆续出版。

中国中央电视台中文国际频道

《快乐中国——学汉语》栏目组

PREFACE

The development of China has attracted the attention of the world, as a result of which a great upsurge for learning Chinese has been going on throughout the world.

The CCTV-4 program *Happy China—Learning Chinese* offers learners an opportunity to learn the Chinese language and culture while enjoying the beautiful scenic spots in China. Co-operating with the local administrations of the well-known scenic spots, this program well combines the learning of language skills with that of Chinese culture and history in an interesting, informative and enjoyable way.

With a 98% coverage in the world, the program of CCTV was broadcast since June, 2004. Quite a lot of the viewers expressed the hope to have the language materials as a learning aid. In view of this, we have invited Beijing Language and Culture University Press, a leading press in publications on Chinese learning materials for foreigners, to produce and publish these language materials for our viewers.

Apart from the language materials presented in the program, Words and Expressions, Notes, Substitution Drills and Conversations are provided in each book, among which Words and Expressions and Notes are accompanied by brief English translations or explanations. Each book is composed of about 15 episodes of the TV program with brief introductions and photos of corresponding scenic spots and travel guides. As more episodes of *Happy China—Learning Chinese* are coming up, more books will be published accordingly.

CCTV-4

Happy China—Learning Chinese Production Team

新 疆

新疆全称为新疆维吾尔自治区，首府为乌鲁木齐市。它地处中国西北部，总面积为166万多平方公里，约占全国总面积的1/6，是中国面积最大、国境线最长、交界邻国最多的省区。汉族、维吾尔族、哈萨克族、回族等将近50个民族生活在那里。新疆深居亚欧大陆腹地,历史上是沟通东西方的“丝绸之路”的要冲，现在又成为横穿两大洲、从中国东海岸的连云港连接荷兰鹿特丹的铁路——第二座“亚欧大陆桥”的必经之地。

新疆风光秀美，组合奇特，雪峰与火洲共存，沙海与绿洲为邻，雪山、草原、沙漠、盆地、河谷等自然景观并存，风貌粗犷，具有边塞特色。著名的自然风景有昭苏草原、唐布拉草原、喀拉峻草原、喀纳斯湖、赛里木湖、喀什河谷。昔日繁华的“丝绸之路”举世闻名，在这里留下了极具文化意味的古城池、古墓葬等历史遗迹，楼兰遗址、香妃墓等蜚声中外，成为了最可宝贵的人文旅游资源。各民族的文化艺术、风情习俗，构成了具有浓郁西部民族特色的旅游人文景观，深受中外游客的喜爱。

本书将向您展开新疆伊犁第一景——果子沟、赛里木湖、喀纳斯湖等迷人的自然风光画卷，带您领略维吾尔族、锡伯族、图瓦族等民族多彩的风俗文化。

不到新疆，不知道山河之美；不到新疆，不知道中国之大。欢迎您走进新疆，体验草原牧民的淳朴生活，感受浪漫多彩的民俗风情。

XINJIANG

Xinjiang, full name Xinjiang Uygur Autonomous Region, is located in northwestern China, and its capital city is Urumchi. With the largest area, the longest borderline and the most neighboring countries in all the province-level administrative regions of China, Xinjiang covers an area of 1.66 million sq. km., taking up about one sixth of Chinese territory. Near 50 nationalities live there, including Han, Uygur, Kazakh, Hui, etc... Situated in the hinterland of Eurasian continent, Xinjiang served as the key controlling section of the well-known "Silk Road" in the past. And now the Second Eurasia Continental Bridge—the railway starting from Lianyungang in China ending at Rotterdam in the Netherlands passes through Xinjiang, making it an important city in connection of the two continents.

Xinjiang boasts gorgeous and unique landscape. Glaciers coexist with volcanoes and vast bodies of sands are adjacent to oases. The coexistence of glaciers, grasslands, deserts, basins, river valleys make Xinjiang full of rough flavor of border area. The famous sights include Zhaosu Grassland, Tangbula Grassland, Kalajun Grassland, Kanas Lake, Salim Lake, and Kashi Valley. The world-known "Silk Road" saw its prosperity in the old times and has left many historical relics such as ancient cities and ancient tombs, among which the ruins of Lou-lan and Abakh Hoja Tomb are the most treasured tourist resources. Different ethnic groups present different cultures, arts and customs with rich ethnic features that attract tourists from both home and abroad.

In this volume, the scroll of the "No.1 Scenery in Ili, Xinjiang" will be unrolled to you: Fruit Gully, Salim Lake, Kanas Lake etc. And we will lead you to experience the colorful local customs of Uygur people, Sibo people and Daur people.

In Xinjiang, you can fully appreciate the beauty of Chinese landscape; in Xinjiang, you can realize how large the territory of China is. Welcome to Xinjiang to experience the simple life of nomadic people and the colorful and romantic local folk customs.

目录
CONTENTS

16
伊犁将军府（第十六集）/ 1

17
伊犁第一景——果子沟（第十七集）/ 15

18
赛里木湖（第十八集）/ 33

19
维吾尔族民居（一）（第十九集）/ 45

20
维吾尔族民居（二）（第二十集）/ 59

21
中哈边界——霍尔果斯口岸（第二十一集）/ 71

22
草原之夜风情园（第二十二集）/ 85

23 林公渠（第二十三集）/ 95

24 锡伯民俗风情园（一）（第二十四集）/ 109

25 锡伯民俗风情园（二）（第二十五集）/ 125

26 喀纳斯湖（一）（第二十六集）/ 139

27 喀纳斯湖（二）（第二十七集）/ 151

28 喀纳斯湖（三）（第二十八集）/ 167

29 喀纳斯湖（四）（第二十九集）/ 179

30 图瓦风情（第三十集）/ 191

伊犁将军府

【第十六集】

场景 Scene 将军府亭子前

大　牛：启禀将军，我们又打了个胜仗。哈哈！果然不出我所料[①]。我伊犁将军，那可真是文才武略，天下无敌，战无不胜！

韩　佳：大牛，一个人演得够带劲儿的呀[②]！还分演了两个角色呢！

大　牛：那是。我牛将军那是学什么像什么[③]！

韩　佳：我看少了一个字，吹牛将军[④]。

大　牛：嗨！

韩　佳：好了，好了。节目开始了。

大　牛：观众朋友们，大家好！200多年前，这里有一座城叫惠远城。今天您就跟着韩佳，还有伊犁将军一起来看看吧！先从这将军府看起[⑤]。

韩　佳：嗬，一口一个伊犁将军[⑥]！那你知道这伊犁将军到底是干什么的吗[⑦]？

大　牛：这伊犁将军嘛，就是……就是将军府的主人呗！

韩　佳：还是我来告诉你吧。你可听好了。

大　牛：请讲，我一定洗耳恭听。

Qǐng jiǎng, wǒ yídìng xǐ ěr gōng tīng.
请 讲，我 一定 洗 耳 恭 听。

Please tell me, I'm all ears.

Daniel: General, we've achieved another victory. Haha! That's exactly what I expected. As General of Ili, I'm a man of both letters and military strategy, invincible and ever-victorious.

Han Jia: Daniel, you are acting alone here so earnestly. And even acting two characters!

Daniel: That's true. I, General Daniel, can play any role.

Han Jia: I think you need one word before your name, "chuiniu jiangjun" (Bragging General).

Daniel: Hey!

Han Jia: So much for it. Our program has started.

Daniel: Hello, everyone. Over 200 years ago, there was a town, called Huiyuan, here. Today, Han Jia and General of Ili will take you there for a look. We'll start right from the General Office.

Han Jia: Huh, you sound like a real general! Then do you know about General of Ili?

Daniel: This General of Ili was the occupant of this General Office.

Han Jia: Let me tell you the details. Listen carefully.

Daniel: Please tell me, I'm all ears.

韩　佳：这伊犁将军全称“总统伊犁等处将军”，是1762年乾隆皇帝[8]设立的。在历史上有57个人担任过这个职位。那当时的惠远城就是第一任伊犁将军组织建造的。

大　牛：明白了，明白了。

韩　佳：明白了？还不随本将军去参观参观将军府。

大　牛：嗨，她也有扮将军的瘾啊！

场景 Scene　将军府内

大　牛：看这将军府啊总感觉有点儿眼熟，好像来到了北京的四合院似的[9]。

韩　佳：的确是这样。这将军府非常有北京建筑的特色。

大　牛：就是嘛。你看这房子坐北朝南，还有这地砖，这房顶，典型的北京四合院，我熟啊！

韩　佳：那不知道这对石狮子你熟不熟啊？

大　牛：这个好像跟北京的石狮子相比还是有一些差别。

韩　佳：差别还不小呢！这对石狮子是非常有地域特色的。

Zhè duì shí shīzi shì fēicháng yǒu dìyù tèsè de.
这 对 石 狮子 是 非常 有 地域 特色 的。

This pair of stone lions has a distinct local flavor.

Han Jia: The full title of the General of Ili was General in Charge of Ili and Other Regions. The position was set by Emperor Qianlong in 1762. Altogether 57 men held the position in history. The former city of Huiyuan was built under the direction of the first General of Ili.

Daniel: Now I see.

Han Jia: You see? Then come with General Han for a tour of the General Office.

Daniel: Hey, she also has a penchant for acting as a general!

Daniel: I find the General Office a bit familiar. It looks like Beijing's traditional courtyard house (*siheyuan*).

Han Jia: Exactly. The General Office shows much of Beijing's architectural style.

Daniel: Yes, indeed. You see, this house also faces south. Its brick floor and rooftop are exactly the same as that of the courtyard houses in Beijing, which I am so familiar with.

Han Jia: Are you also familiar with this pair of stone lions?

Daniel: These stone lions look a bit different from those I've seen in Beijing.

Han Jia: A lot more different. This pair of stone lions has a distinct local flavor.

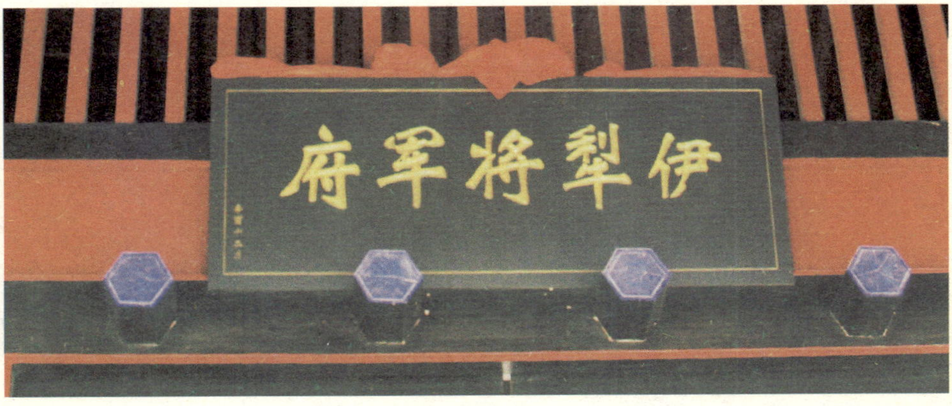

场景 Scene　将军府内

韩　佳：这将军府所在的惠远城，在很长一段历史时期内都是新疆政治、经济、文化的中心。

大　牛：我听说当时城内非常繁华，有“小北京”之称[10]。

韩　佳：是啊，惠远城当时是新疆的第一大城。

大　牛：这么大的一座城市我们肯定要逛个三五天才能逛完呢。

韩　佳：想逛三五天可以，你要是想快快地看也可以。有一个地方可以把惠远城尽收眼底。

大　牛：尽收眼底啊？得，不用说了。又要吭哧吭哧往高处爬了。哎，韩佳，今天是爬山啊，还是登塔啊？

场景 Scene　钟鼓楼下

韩　佳：今天啊，我们要爬楼。

大　牛：爬楼？

韩　佳：对啊，就是惠远古城的钟鼓楼。

大　牛：原来是钟鼓楼啊！中国的很多城市都有。我见得可多了。

韩　佳：这惠远古城的钟鼓楼跟别处的可不一样。

大　牛：怎么讲？

韩　佳：想知道啊？先爬楼。

大　牛：走吧！

Han Jia: Huiyuan, the seat of the General Office, for a long period of time was the political, economic and cultural center of Xinjiang.

Daniel: I heard it was quite a prosperous city then, said to be "Little Beijing".

Han Jia: Yes. Huiyuan was then Xinjiang's largest city.

Daniel: It will take us at least three to five days to complete a tour of such a large city.

Han Jia: You may stroll here for three to five days. But you can also see it very briefly. There is a vantage point where you can have a bird's-eye view of the city.

Daniel: A bird's-eye view? You don't have to tell me where. I know we'll huff and puff again to climb a high place. Eh, Han Jia, are we going to climb a mountain or a tower today?

Han Jia: Today we're going to climb a tower.

Daniel: A tower?

Han Jia: Yes, the Bell and Drum Tower of Huiyuan.

Daniel: Oh, the Bell and Drum Tower. There are such towers in many other Chinese cities. I've seen a lot of them.

Han Jia: But this Bell and Drum Tower of Huiyuan is different from those in other cities.

Daniel: What do you mean?

Han Jia: You want to know? Climb the tower first.

Daniel: Let's go.

场景 Scene 钟鼓楼上

韩　佳：大牛，这钟鼓楼的特别之处就在于它在整座城的正中心[11]。

大　牛：哦，钟鼓楼在惠远古城的正中心。

韩　佳：没错儿。你看，钟鼓楼东南西北的四座门正对着四条大路。

Zhōnggǔ Lóu de sì zuò mén zhèng duìzhe sì tiáo dà lù.
钟鼓 楼 的 四 座 门 正 对着 四 条 大 路。

The four gates of the Bell and Drum Tower are in line with the four large roads.

大　牛：是吗？我试试。

韩　佳：真服了你了！

大　牛：嗯，经过我的精确测量发现……

韩　佳：发现什么？

大　牛：这四座大门的确正对着四个方向。

韩　佳：咳，这还用你说啊？不过可惜的是，这钟啊，鼓啊，现在已经不复存在了[12]。

大　牛：是挺可惜的！“不复存在”中的“复”是什么意思？

韩　佳：“不复存在”中的“复”是“再、又”的意思。“不复存在”就是说以前有但现在不存在，不再有了。

大　牛：不复存在。不过没关系。

韩　佳：哎呀，你乱敲什么啊？

大　牛：谁乱敲了？我在报时啊。

韩　佳：报时？

大　牛：对啊，我在提醒大家现在又到“赏心悦目”的时间了。

Han Jia: Daniel, the unusualness of this Huiyuan tower is that it stands in the center of the city.

Daniel: Oh, the tower lies in the city center.

Han Jia: Exactly. You see, the four gates of the Bell and Drum Tower are in line with the four large roads.

Daniel: Really? Let me see.

Han Jia: You are fantastic!

Daniel: After my precise surveys ...

Han Jia: What have you found?

Daniel: The four gates exactly face four directions.

Han Jia: Hey, that's needless to say. But it's a pity the bell and the drum are no longer in existence here.

Daniel: A pity indeed! What does the "fu" in "bu fu cunzai" mean?

Han Jia: "Fu" means "again" or "still". "Bu fu cunzai" means what existed before no longer exists.

Daniel: But that doesn't matter.

Han Jia: Hey, why are you making such a noise?

Daniel: I'm making no noise. I'm telling the time.

Han Jia: Telling the time?

Daniel: Yeah, I am reminding our audience that it's time again to enjoy the *Enjoyable Scenery*.

生 词 Words and Expressions

1. 文才武略		wén cái wǔ luè	literary talent and military ability
2. 洗耳恭听		xǐ ěr gōng tīng	to listen with respectful attention
3. 建造	（动）	jiànzào	to build; construct; make
4. 眼熟	（形）	yǎnshú	familiar
5. 特色	（名）	tèsè	characteristic; distinctive feature
6. 坐北朝南		zuò běi cháo nán	to face south
7. 典型	（名、形）	diǎnxíng	typical case, model, type; typical, representative
8. 繁华	（形）	fánhuá	flourishing; bustling; busy
9. 尽收眼底		jìn shōu yǎn dǐ	to have a panoramic view
10. 测量	（动）	cèliáng	to survey; measure; gauge

注 释 Notes

1. 果然不出我所料。

“果然”，副词，表示事实跟所说的或所预料的情况相符合。

The adverb “果然” is used to indicate that the fact itself accords with what has been said or expected.

例如：听说杭州西湖的景色很美，到那一看果然不错。

“所”，助词，“所＋动词”构成名词性短语。“不出我所料”即“不出我预料的情况”。

The particle “所” is used to form the nominal phrase “所 + verb”. “不出我所料” means “as what I expected”.

例如：据我所知，这件事情已经解决了。

2. 一个人演得够带劲儿的呀！

“带劲儿”，动词，这里指有劲头儿，非常投入。多用于口语。

The verb “带劲儿” here means “energetic; devoted”. It is often used in spoken Chinese.

例如：他唱歌唱得真带劲儿。

3. 我牛将军那是学什么像什么！

“……什么……什么”，“什么”，疑问代词，句中两个“什么”前后照应，表示前者决定后者。

In the construction“……什么……什么”，“什么”is an interrogative pronoun, the former“什么”determines the latter.

例如：他做什么咱们就吃什么。

4. 我看少了一个字，吹牛将军。

“吹牛”也说吹牛皮，意思是夸口，说大话。

“吹牛” or“吹牛皮” means “to boast; talk big”.

例如：他这个人就喜欢吹牛。

5. 先从这将军府看起。

“从……起”，表示开始时间或起点的范围。

The construction“从……起”indicates the starting time or starting point.

例如：从明天起学校正式开学上课。

保护环境要从自己做起。

6. 一口一个伊犁将军！

“一口一个……”，表示说话中反复不断地提到某人某事，带有夸张。用于口语。

例如：你看你一口一个小张，总是忘不了她。

The colloquial expression“一口一个……”, with a tone of exaggeration, indicates that a speaker has been repeatedly mentioning somebody or something.

7. 那你知道这伊犁将军到底是干什么的吗？

“到底”，副词，用在疑问句里，表示进一步追究。

The adverb“到底”is used in an interrogative sentence to indicate further inquiry.

例如：你到底去不去？

8. 乾隆皇帝

乾隆皇帝：中国历史上清代的一位皇帝，年号为乾隆，在位时间为 1736 年到 1795 年。

Emperor Qianlong was an emperor of the Qing Dynasty in Chinese history. He was on the throne from 1736 to 1795 and the title of his reign was Qianlong.

9. 好像来到了北京的四合院似的。

“似的”，助词，用在名词、代词或动词后，表示跟某种事物或情况相似。前面常用“像、好像”搭配。

The particle “似的” is used after a noun, pronoun or verb to indicate that something or a situation is similar to another one. And it often precedes with “像” or “好像”.

例如：我进去时，他好像睡着了似的。

10. 我听说当时城内非常繁华，有“小北京”之称。

“之”，是古汉语遗留下来的结构助词，用法相当于现代汉语中的“的”字。这里表示修饰关系。“……之称”即“……的称呼”。用于书面语。

“之”, whose usage is equivalent to that of “的” in modern Chinese, is a structural particle left over from classical Chinese. In this sentence，it is used to show modification. “……之称” means “the title of ...”. And it is used in written Chinese.

例如：这是一件无价之宝。

11. 这钟鼓楼的特别之处就在于它在整座城的正中心。

“在于”，动词，正是，就是；指出事物的本质所在。

The verb “在于” means “to rest with; lie in; consist in”, pointing out the essence of something.

例如：他学习成绩下降的原因在于他大部分精力没放在学习上。

12. 不过可惜的是，这钟啊，鼓啊，现在已经不复存在了。

“不过”，连词，表示转折，这里用来补充、修正上文的意思。比“但是”轻，多用于口语。

The conjunction “不过”, indicating transition, is used here to complement and revise what has been said above. It is weaker than “但是” in degree and is mostly used in oral Chinese.

例如：小王工作很努力，不过性子太急。

"啊"，助词，用在句中停顿的地方，表示列举。

The particle "啊" is used in a pause of the sentence to enumerate items.

例如：这里的山啊，水啊，树啊，草啊，都是那么漂亮。

替换练习 Substitution Drills

1. 请讲，我一定	洗耳恭听。
	虚心接受
	认真考虑
	严肃处理

2. 这	对	石狮子	是非常有	地域	特色的。
	座	古建筑		西方	
	尊	玉佛像		中国	
	套	木家具		欧洲	

3. 钟鼓楼	的	四座	门正对着	四条大路。
学校		西南		一个商场
颐和园		东宫		一片树林
故宫		后		景山公园

会 话 Conversations

完成下列会话 Complete the following dialogues
（如括号里有词语或提示，请按要求做 Use the words or expressions given in the brackets）

A: 这个将军府怎么有点儿像北京的四合院？
B: ______________________________。（果然）
A: 我们进去参观参观吧。
B: ______________________________。（从……起）

A: 这个建筑有什么特色呢？
B: ______________________________。（在于）
A: 这钟鼓楼里面的钟啊，鼓啊，还都在吗？
B: ______________________________。（不复存在）

伊犁第一景——果子沟
【第十七集】

场景 Scene 果子沟

韩　佳：这里呢，就是我们今天学汉语的地方——果子沟。它可号称“伊犁第一景”呢。每天都有不少人要到这里来。哎，我前面就有一位，牵着毛驴、看着美景，还真惬意！怎么看着像大牛啊？

场景 Scene 盘山路上

韩　佳：大牛，真是你啊！

大　牛：韩佳，你看我像不像新疆传奇的人物——阿凡提啊？

韩　佳：啊，阿凡提？哦，像，还真像！

大　牛：那是。我跟阿凡提那可都是聪明绝顶的人物啊！

Wǒmen dōu shì cōngming juédǐng de rénwù.
我们　都　是　聪明　绝顶　的　人物。

We are both incredibly intelligent people.

Han Jia: Here is the place where we're going to learn Chinese today, Fruit Gully. It is claimed as the "No.1 Sight in Ili". There are many visitors here every day. Hey, there's someone before me, leading a donkey while enjoying the scenery. What a carefree man! Why, he looks like Daniel!

Daniel: Daniel, is it really you?

Daniel: Han Jia, do you think I look like Xinjiang's legendary figure Afanti?

Han Jia: Ah, Afanti? Uh, you do look like him.

Daniel: Sure. Both Afanti and I are extremely intelligent.

大　牛：“聪明绝顶”，*就是形容非常聪明。*

韩　佳：这种词语他倒学得快。“绝顶”就是极端、非常的意思。“聪明绝顶”就是形容某个人非常地聪明。

大　牛：没错儿。韩佳，聪明绝顶的人在这儿呢！你老看着我的驴干吗呀？

韩　佳：咳，我是说这驴跟阿凡提的那头驴特别像。

大　牛：啊，光驴像啊？

韩　佳：你以为呢？

大　牛：咳，你是嫉妒我的驴，还是嫉妒我呢？

韩　佳：啊？

大　牛：我们骑驴看唱本——走着瞧[1]！走，看果子沟去。我有一头小毛驴，从来也不骑。

Daniel: "Congming jueding" is an expression which means "extremely intelligent".

Han Jia: He learns such phrases fast. "Jueding" means extreme or exceptional. "Congming jueding" means extremely intelligent.

Daniel: Exactly. Han Jia, the extremely intelligent man is here. Why are you always staring at my donkey?

Han Jia: Hey, I mean this donkey looks like Afanti's donkey.

Daniel: Ah, only the donkey is a look-alike?

Han Jia: What else do you think?

Daniel: Hey, you are jealous of my donkey and also jealous of me.

Han Jia: What?

Daniel: Let's wait and see. Let's go see the Fruit Gully. I have a little donkey, but I never ride it.

场景 Scene 瀑布

韩　佳：大牛，你这小毛驴好像不听话呀。

大　牛：谁说的？我让它往东，它不敢往西。你听着！你给我站着不许动！

韩　佳：你别说，它还挺会挑地方。这瀑布可是果子沟的一景。

大　牛：虽然这瀑布的水势不大，但是有旁边的青草绿树，还有枯木点缀，真是有意境[2]。有意境。

韩　佳：这瀑布是挺有意境的。

Zhè pùbù shì tǐng yǒu yìjìng de.
这　瀑布　是　挺　有　意境　的。

This waterfall has a certain essence.

韩　佳：这瀑布是挺有意境的，可你不觉得你少了点儿什么吗？

大　牛：啊，你给我站住！哎，你回来！

Han Jia: Daniel, your donkey doesn't seem quite tame.

Daniel: That's not true. If I want it to go east, it won't go west. Listen to me. Stay put!

Han Jia: It is surely good at choosing places. The waterfall here is a scenic spot of the gully.

Daniel: Although the fall isn't so big, with the grass and trees studded with withered trunks and branches on both sides, it is really poetic. Quite poetic.

Han Jia: This waterfall has a certain essence.

Han Jia: The waterfall is poetic indeed, but don't you think something is missing?

Daniel: Hey, halt! Hey, come back!

场景 Scene 云杉林

大　牛：看你这回还往哪儿跑！我要把你拴起来。

韩　佳：大牛，你可够快的呀！比我还早到，先到云杉林了。

大　牛：云杉啊？哦，对。你看这云杉长得多么厚实啊！一大片一大片的，真漂亮！

韩　佳：哎，形容事物之间的距离近、空隙小，要用密或者紧密。可不能用厚实。

大　牛："密"和"紧密"表示事物之间的距离近、空隙小。哎，韩佳，我还发现了一个问题。

韩　佳：哦，什么问题啊？

大　牛：你说这云杉笔直笔直的，层次分明，像不像这新疆维吾尔族特有的图案？

韩　佳：哎，还真有那么点儿意思！

大　牛：我今天才发现，这种花纹简直是云杉林的抽象画③。从这里欣赏果子沟的美景真是太壮观了！

韩　佳：是啊。

Daniel: You'll go nowhere. I'll keep you tethered.

Han Jia: Daniel, you are so fast. You've reached the spruce forest earlier than I.

Daniel: Spruces? Oh, yeah, yeah. Look how "houshi" the spruces are! Such a large spruce forest! So beautiful!

Han Jia: Hey, when you describe things that are close together, you should use "mi" (dense) or "jinmi" (very dense). You shouldn't use "houshi" (thick and solid).

Daniel: "Mi", fourth tone, and "jinmi" both mean "dense". Eh, Han Jia, I have another discovery.

Han Jia: What is it?

Daniel: Do you think the upright spruce with clear layers of leaves resembles the patterns peculiar to the Uygur people of Xinjiang?

Han Jia: Yeah, sort of.

Daniel: I've just realized that this kind of floral patterns is an abstract painting of the spruce forest. Stand here, you'll find the Fruit Gully so impressive.

Han Jia: Yes, indeed.

场景 Scene 观景台

韩　佳：这么美的果子沟，自古以来还是新疆通往中亚、欧亚“丝绸之路”的关口呢[4]！

大　牛：哎呀，伊犁这道天然的大门真够漂亮的！

韩　佳：可不是嘛[5]！

大　牛：韩佳，那边是什么植物啊？

韩　佳：那些是人工种植的云杉。别看它们现在小，将来也能长成参天大树。

大　牛：这俗话说得好：“十年树木，百年树人。”

Shí nián shù mù, bǎi nián shù rén.
十　年　树　木，百　年　树　人。

It takes ten years to grow trees but one hundred years to cultivate people.

韩　佳：这云杉长得可慢了，十年可成不了材。

大　牛：我的驴呢？

Han Jia: This beautiful Fruit Gully in ancient times was a pass of the Silk Road that led to Central Asia and Europe.

Daniel: Wow, this natural gateway of Ili is so beautiful!

Han Jia: Yes, indeed.

Daniel: Han Jia, what are those plants over there?

Han Jia: Those are planted spruces. Although they are short, they'll grow into towering big trees one day.

Daniel: Just as the saying goes: "It takes ten years to grow trees, but one hundred years to cultivate people."

Han Jia: Spruce trees grow very slowly. A ten-year-old spruce couldn't become good timber.

Daniel: Where's my donkey?

场景 Scene 野果林

大　牛：哎呀，可找着你了！刚才你跑哪儿去了呢？

韩　佳：大牛，这小毛驴终于听你的话了⑥。

大　牛：就是。

韩　佳：可是你带着它转什么圈啊？

大　牛：其实我是想在这里摘一点儿野果，正好它可以帮我们运回去。

韩　佳：那倒也是⑦。这果子沟本来就是以满山的野果而得名的⑧。那你去摘吧！

大　牛：就是，就是。我们俩各有分工。你负责带观众朋友们赏美景，我负责给大家摘野果，尝个新鲜嘛！

韩　佳：没问题！大家跟我走，我们去看一看果子沟赏心悦目的美景吧！

Daniel: Aha, I've finally found you. Where were you just now?

Han Jia: Daniel, this little donkey has finally become obedient to you.

Daniel: Yes.

Han Jia: But why did you take him with you around here?

Daniel: Actually, I want to pick some wild berries to take on his back.

Han Jia: That's reasonable. The Fruit Gully got its name just because of the wild berries growing all over the mountain. Then pick your berries.

Daniel: Sure. But we have to divide the work between us. You are responsible for showing our audience the scenery. And I am responsible for picking berries for everyone to taste.

Han Jia: No problem. Les's enjoy the beautiful scenery in Fruit Gully.

生 词 Words and Expressions

1. 号称	（动）	hàochēng	to be known as
2. 惬意	（形）	qièyì	to be pleased; be satisfied
3. 传奇	（名）	chuánqí	legend
4. 点缀	（动）	diǎnzhuì	to embellish
5. 意境	（名）	yìjìng	essence
6. 空隙	（名）	kòngxì	space; gap; interval
7. 图案	（名）	tú'àn	pattern; design
8. 抽象	（形）	chōuxiàng	abstract
9. 壮观	（形）	zhuàngguān	grand; magnificent
10. 参天大树		cāntiān dà shù	towering tree

注 释 Notes

1. 我们骑驴看唱本——走着瞧！

“骑驴看唱本——走着瞧”是一句歇后语。歇后语是由两个部分组成的一句话，前部分比喻或说出一件事情，像谜面；后部分说出本意，像谜底。这句歇后语的前部分是“骑驴看唱本”，后部分是“走着瞧”，意思是在事物的发展过程中看出结果。“瞧”的表面意思是看、读，实际的意思是观察并加以判断。

“骑驴看唱本——走着瞧”is a“歇后语”.“歇后语”is a two-part allegorical saying, of which the first part, always stated, is descriptive, while the second part, sometimes unstated, carries the message. In this allegorical saying, the first part is“骑驴看唱本”and the second part is“走着瞧”. It means“the result will be seen in the process of the development of something”.“瞧”literally means“to read”and actually means“to observe and judge”.

2. 虽然这瀑布的水势不大，但是有旁边的青草绿树，还有枯木点缀，真是有意境。

“虽然……但是……”，这是一个转折复句结构。“虽然”，连词，表示让步，承认某件事为事实，但另一件事并不因此而不成立。后一小句常用“但是、可是、还是、可、却”等呼应。

"虽然……但是……" is a pattern of transitional compound sentence. The conjunction "虽然" indicates concession, acknowledging that one thing is a fact, but the other thing is not untenable because of that. At the beginning of the latter clause, there is usually "但是", "可是", "还是", "可" or "却" collocating with "虽然".

例如：这所学校虽然名气不大，但是教学质量很高。

3. 这种花纹简直是云杉林的抽象画。

"简直"，副词，表示强调夸大的语气，说明事情或状态达到很高的程度。

The adverb "简直" is used to express an exaggerated tone and indicate that a kind of thing or state has reached a great extent.

例如：你变化真大，我简直认不出你来了。

4. 这么美的果子沟，自古以来还是新疆通往中亚、欧亚"丝绸之路"的关口呢！

"……以来"，表示从过去某时直到说话时（或特指的某一时间）为止的一段时间。也说成"从（自从）……以来"。

"……以来" or "从（自从）……以来", equivalent to "since" in English, means from sometime in the past until now or a specific time.

例如：自开学以来，我就没有进过城。

丝绸之路：古代横贯亚洲的大通道，东起中国的渭水流域，西至地中海东岸及罗马各地。自西汉以后一千多年间，大量的中国丝及丝织品都经过这条通道运到西方，故称"丝绸之路"。

The Silk Road is a passageway traversing Asia in ancient times, beginning from the Wei River Valley of China and ending at the east shore of the Mediterranean Sea and some places of Rome. During the 1,000 odd years after the Western Han Dynasty, a lot of silk and silk fabrics were carried from China to the West through this passage, and therefore it was called the Silk Road.

5. 可不是嘛！

"可不是嘛"，表示同意某人说的话。

"可不是嘛", indicates agreement with somebody.

例如：A：今年的冬天一点儿也不冷。

B：可不是嘛，到十一月了还这样暖和。

6. 大牛，这小毛驴终于听你的话了。

"终于"，表示经过较长过程后愿望实现了。

"终于"，indicates that one's wish has come true at last.

例如：经过几年的努力，试验终于成功了。

7. 那倒也是。

"倒"，副词，用于交谈中肯定对方。

The adverb "倒" is used in a dialogue to approve of what the other side has said.

例如：A：我不想出国留学，想在国内继续工作。

B：那倒也好，能有现在这份工作也不容易。

8. 这果子沟本来就是以满山的野果而得名的。

"以"，介词，这里用来表示原因，后面可以用连词"而"把前面表示原因的成分连接到动词上面。

The preposition "以" is used to indicate reason and it can collocate with the conjunction "而" connecting the element denoting reason with the verb.

例如：这所学校以教学质量高而闻名全国。

替换练习 Substitution Drills

1. 我们都是 聪明绝顶 的人物。
   - 智慧超常
   - 财富亿万
   - 学识渊博

2. 这 瀑布 是挺有 意境 的。
   - 诗歌 …… 韵味
   - 作品 …… 意义
   - 油画 …… 味道

会话 Conversations

完成下列会话 Complete the following dialogues

（**如括号里有词语或提示，请按要求做** Use the words or expressions given in the brackets）

A: 这里的风景实在太美了！

B: ______________________________！（简直）

A: 这样美丽的景色以前我们只在电视中看过。

B: ______________________________。（可不是）

A: 这里为什么叫葡萄沟呢？

B: ______________________________。（以……而……）

A: 下次我们把孩子也带来玩儿几天。

B: ______________________________。（其实）

赛里木湖

【第十八集】

场景 Scene 赛里木湖边

韩　佳：还没有下车啊，就被这片蓝蓝的湖水所吸引。赛里木湖比我想象的还要宽阔，还要美。哎，好像有人比我来得还早。

场景 Scene 赛里木湖前

韩　佳：大牛，大牛，你发什么呆啊①？

大　牛：嘘！

韩　佳：你是在欣赏赛里木湖，这么出神？

大　牛：别吵！我在等天鹅。

韩　佳：等天鹅？

大　牛：当地居民跟我说，赛里木湖上会出现天鹅。要是我在这里耐心等待的话，就很可能遇见天鹅②。

韩　佳：咳，这湖面会出现天鹅倒是真的，但是这种场景是可遇而不可求的。你这么干等也不是办法呀。

Nǐ zhème gān děng yě bú shì bànfǎ ya.
你这么干等也不是办法呀。

It's no good for you just to sit here waiting.

大　牛：也许别人不行，我大牛一定能等到。

Han Jia: While I'm still in the car, I'm already attracted by the azure lake over there. Salim Lake is much wider and more beautiful than I expected. Hey, someone came here even earlier than me.

Han Jia: Daniel, Daniel, What are you staring at?

Daniel: Sh!

Han Jia: Are you enjoying Salim Lake so attentively?

Daniel: Quiet! I'm waiting for swans.

Han Jia: Waiting for swans?

Daniel: Local people told me there would be swans on Salim Lake. If I wait here patiently, I may have a chance to see them.

Han Jia: Hey, it's true that swans have appeared on the lake, but a situation like that occurs only by chance. It's no good for you just to sit here waiting.

Daniel: Maybe others aren't so lucky. I am sure I may see them.

场景 Scene 赛里木湖边

韩 佳：这个大牛只顾等天鹅，连节目都不管了③。那我只能一个人带您转转了。这赛里木湖是新疆最大的高山湖泊。

大 牛：没错儿。传说中湖里的水就是一对恋人的泪水汇集而成的，这湖啊……

韩 佳：哎，大牛，你不是要等天鹅吗？

大 牛：天鹅要等，这风景也要看嘛。你看，这里山清水秀的。即使没有天鹅的光临，景色也是非常迷人的。

韩 佳：那倒是。你看，远处有雪山，近处有湖水。翠绿的云杉前还有袅袅的炊烟。

大 牛：鸟，在哪儿啊？没有碰到天鹅，要是能看见鸟也行啊。

韩 佳：咳，你说什么呢？我说的是袅袅炊烟。"袅袅"是个形容词，用来形容烟雾缭绕上升的样子。跟飞的鸟没什么关系。

大 牛：哦，我明白了。"袅袅"，*读三声，是个形容词，用来形容烟雾缭绕上升的样子。*袅袅。我是太想看到天鹅。

Wǒ shì tài xiǎng kàndào tiān'é.
我 是 太 想 看到 天鹅。

I want so much to see swans.

Han Jia: He only cares about the swans. He has forgotten our program. So I have to take our viewers on the tour alone. Salim Lake is the largest mountain lake in Xinjiang.

Daniel: Exactly. It's said the water in the lake came from the tears of two lovers. Oh, this lake...

Han Jia: Hey, Daniel, weren't you waiting for the swans?

Daniel: But the scenery is also worth seeing while waiting for the swans. Look at the green mountains and the blue lake. Despite the absence of swans, the scenery is already mesmerizing.

Han Jia: That's true. There are snow-capped mountains in the distance and a lake nearby. "Niaoniao" (curling wisps of) smoke rises in front of the green spruce trees.

Daniel: Where are the birds? It wouldn't be bad to see some birds if no swans are here.

Han Jia: Hey, what are you talking about? What I said was "niaoniao chui yan". "Niaoniao" is an adjective, used to describe curling wisps of smoke. It has nothing to do with the flying birds.

Daniel: Oh, I see. "Niaoniao", two third tones, is an adjective, which is used to describe a wisp of smoke curling up into the heavens. I want so much to see swans.

场景 Scene 赛里木湖前

韩　佳：大牛，大牛，这湖在后边呢！你冲这边发什么呆啊[4]？

大　牛：嘘！

韩　佳：天鹅不会来这儿的。

大　牛：谁等天鹅了？我是担心你打扰我的羊吃草。

韩　佳：啊，这是你的羊？

大　牛：人家让我帮忙放会儿羊。

韩　佳：放牧可是很专业的工作。你行吗？

大　牛：我行吗？看来我不给你展示展示，你也不服啊[5]。看我的！

韩　佳：好！

大　牛：来来来！集合！集合！

韩　佳：大牛，这是你的羊吗？你不会认错了吧？

大　牛：没错儿啊。哎呀，算了，算了[6]。差不多就行了。一会儿把羊交给它们的主人，就完事大吉[7]。

韩　佳：啊，不会吧？就这么草草了事了。

大　牛：“草草……”好像是一个跟草有关的成语。韩佳是夸我呢，还是贬我呢？

Tā shì kuā wǒ ne, háishi biǎn wǒ ne?
她是夸我呢，还是贬我呢？

Is she complimenting me or mocking me?

Han Jia: Daniel, the lake is behind us, why are you staring blankly over there?

Daniel: Sh!

Han Jia: Swans won't come here.

Daniel: I'm not waiting for swans. I am worrying you may disturb my grazing sheep.

Han Jia: What, your sheep?

Daniel: The sheep someone asked me to take care of.

Han Jia: Herding sheep is a professional job. You think you are up to it?

Daniel: Am I up to it? If I don't show my skills, you won't believe me. Just watch.

Han Jia: Okay.

Daniel: Come on! Get together now!

Han Jia: Daniel, are they the sheep you are supposed to take care of? You may be dealing with a wrong flock.

Daniel: I can't be wrong. Oh, forget it. It's almost done. In a moment, I'll just give them back to their owner. And it's all done.

Han Jia: Oh, no. You can't "caocao liao shi" like this.

Daniel: "Caocao" seems to be an idiom related with grass. Is Han Jia complimenting me or mocking me?

韩　佳：这里的“草”是草率、马虎的意思。“草草了事”这个成语，就是说马马虎虎地就把事情办完了，形容办得很不彻底、很不认真。

大　牛：“草草了事”*这个成语就是说马马虎虎地就把事情办完了*。草草了事。得，我啊还是放我的羊去吧。韩佳，我要是放得好的话，你得给我找一个褒义的成语夸我。

韩　佳：知道了。那咱们也别干等着了，一起来看看今天的“赏心悦目”。

Han Jia: "Cao" here means rash and careless. "Caocao liao shi", as an idiom, means "to do something rashly and carelessly", implying an irresponsible and careless attitude.

Daniel: "Caocao liao shi" is a Chinese idiom which means "to be careless or hurried about doing things". Okay, I'd better go on herding my sheep. Han Jia, if I herd my sheep well, you must use a commendatory idiom to praise me.

Han Jia: Yeah, I will. Then we'd better stop waiting and move on to today's *Enjoyable Scenery*.

生词 Words and Expressions

1. 吸引	（动）	xīyǐn	to attract; draw; fascinate
2. 湖泊	（名）	húpō	lakes
3. 汇集	（动）	huìjí	to compile; collect; converge
4. 山清水秀		shān qīng shuǐ xiù	green hills and clear waters — picturesque scenery
5. 翠绿	（形）	cuìlǜ	emerald green; jade green
6. 缭绕	（动）	liáorào	to curl up; wind around
7. 展示	（动）	zhǎnshì	to display
8. 草率	（形）	cǎoshuài	sloppy; careless
9. 马虎	（形）	mǎhu	careless; casual
10. 褒义	（名）	bāoyì	commendatory sense

注释 Notes

1. 你发什么呆啊？

“什么”，代词，在动词后表示不满。“发呆”为动宾结构，“什么”放在中间表示对“发呆”的不满。

The pronoun “什么” is used after a verb to express dissatisfaction. “发呆” is a construction of “verb+object” and “什么” is placed in between to express dissatisfaction at “发呆”.

例如：你看什么电视，该学习了。

2. 要是我在这里耐心等待的话，就很可能遇见天鹅。

“要是……的话”，也说成“要……的话”，和“要是”的用法基本一样，用于口语。“要是”，连词，表示假设，和“如果、假如”意思基本相同。“要是……的话”后面常有“就、也”呼应。

The colloquial expression “要是……的话” or “要……的话” used in spoken Chinese is basically equivalent to “如果” or “假如” in meaning. It indicates assumption and often collocates with “就” or “也” in the latter part of the sentence. And its usage is basically the same as that of “要是”.

例如：要是下雨的话，我们就不出去了。

3. 连节目都不管了。

“连……都（也）……”，这一结构常用来表示强调。所要强调的成分放在“连……都（也）”的中间。

The construction “连……都(也)……” is often used for emphasis. And what is to be emphasized is put between “连” and “都（也）”.

例如：你在北京住了那么多年，连长城都没去过？

4. 你冲这边发什么呆啊？

“冲”，动词，这里的意思是向着或对着。用于口语。

The verb “冲” means “facing; towards” and is used in colloquial Chinese.

例如：你这话是冲我来的。

5. 看来我不给你展示展示，你也不服啊。

“看来”，这里是插入语，表示根据客观情况估计。

“看来” here is a parenthesis, meaning “to estimate according to the objective condition”.

例如：雨这么大，看来他回不来了。

6. 哎呀，算了，算了。

“算了”，作罢，事情不再进行下去。

“算了” means “to forget it; let it go”.

例如：算了，别再说了。

7. 一会儿把羊交给它们的主人，就完事大吉。

“大吉”，意思是非常吉利。用在动词或动词结构后，是一种诙谐的说法。

“大吉”, meaning “very lucky; highly auspicious”, is used after a verb or a verb phrase to show humor.

例如：商店生意不好，一直亏损，最后只好关门大吉。

替换练习 Substitution Drills

1. 你这么 干等 也不是办法呀。
   - 哭下去
   - 熬夜
   - 不吃不喝

2. 我是太想 看到 天鹅。
   - 出国 留学
   - 回家 过年

3. 她是 夸 我呢，还是 贬 我呢？
   - 表扬 批评
   - 爱 恨
   - 帮 害

会 话 Conversations

完成下列会话 Complete the following dialogues

（如括号里有词语或提示，请按要求做 Use the words or expressions given in the brackets）

A: 天鹅长什么样子？

B: ________________________。（连……都……）

A: 是的，我没见过天鹅，但我看过芭蕾舞《天鹅湖》。

B: ________________________。（……什么）

A: 这里的环境真好。

B: ________________________。（要是）

A: 你愿意把家搬到这里来？

B: ________________________。（不过）

维吾尔族民居（一）

【第十九集】

场景 Scene 维吾尔族民居前

韩　佳：大家好，欢迎如约来到《快乐中国》！我是快乐的韩佳。看见我身后这漂亮的民居了吗？今天啊，我就要去拜访一下这家的主人。

大　牛：欢迎大家到我家来做客！

韩　佳：谢谢，谢谢啊。维吾尔族的朋友就是热情好客。

大　牛：我们维吾尔族小伙子，除了热情好客以外，还特别英俊潇洒①。您瞧我的小花帽，我的花衬衫。

韩　佳：哎！下次把胡子粘好了再出来。

大　牛：没问题。什么胶水啊！

场景 Scene 葡萄架下

韩　佳：大牛，你看！那就是典型的维吾尔族民居。蓝色和白色是维吾尔族朋友特别喜欢的两种颜色。

大　牛：好大一片葡萄架子呀！

韩　佳：哎，你别忘了，葡萄是新疆的特产。在新疆，几乎每家的院子里都有葡萄架。

Zài Xīnjiāng, jīhū měi jiā de yuànzi li dōu yǒu pútáojià.
在新疆，几乎每家的院子里都有葡萄架。

In Xinjiang, the courtyard of almost every home has a grape trellis.

Han Jia: Hello, welcome to *Happy China*! I am happy Han Jia. Do you see this nice house behind me? Today, I'm going to visit the owner of this house.

Daniel: Welcome to my home!

Han Jia: Thank you very much. Uygur friends are so warm and hospitable.

Daniel: We Uygur young men are not only warm and hospitable, but also handsome and elegant. Look at my embellished cap and my figured shirt.

Han Jia: Oh! Next time stick your moustache firmly before coming out.

Daniel: No problem. What bad glue it is!

Han Jia: Daniel, look. That is a typical Uygur dwelling. Blue and white are the two favorite colors of Uygur people.

Daniel: Wow, what a sprawling grape trellis!

Han Jia: Yeah, don't forget the grape is a special local product of Xinjiang. In Xinjiang, there is a grape trellis in the courtyard of almost every home.

嘉　宾：欢迎！欢迎！

大　牛：哎呀，好多的麻花……

韩　佳：啊？

大　牛：……辫子。

韩　佳：麻花辫子几乎是维吾尔族姑娘的象征了。有特点吧？

大　牛：太有特点了。

嘉　宾：大牛，你刚一进来就说到我们维族的三大特色。嗯，漂亮的房子，满院的葡萄架子，还有姑娘的辫子。

大　牛：其实这个不算什么。我对新疆的文化特别感兴趣，自己也做了一些研究。

韩　佳：哎，打住，打住！怎么刚夸你几句，就开始吹上牛了呀！还是赶快带我们去参观一下你们漂亮的家吧！

嘉　宾：好啊！

大　牛：哎，但是从哪儿看起啊？我们要看最有特色的。

嘉　宾：俗话说民以食为天②，要不然我们先去看看新疆特色的食品吧！

合：好啊。

大　牛：这个我喜欢。

嘉　宾：请！

Guest: Welcome! Welcome!

Daniel: Wow, so many dough twists!

Han Jia: What?

Daniel: Plaits.

Han Jia: The dough-twist style plaits are a symbol of Uygur girls. Are they special?

Daniel: Oh, very much.

Guest: Daniel, soon after we came in, you mentioned three features of the Uygur people—a pretty house, a whole yard of grape trellis and the girls' plaits.

Daniel: But those are no surprise to me. The culture of Xinjiang interests me very much. And I've also done some research.

Han Jia: Hey, stop, stop! Soon after I said a few nice words about you, you began talking big. Please show us your pretty house now.

Guest: Okay.

Daniel: Oh, where should we start? We want to see the most special parts.

Guest: As a saying goes: "food is the paramount necessity of the people." How about seeing the Xinjiang cuisine first?

Together: Good idea.

Daniel: I like it.

Guest: Please.

场景 Scene 院子里

大 牛：怎么都是原料啊？

嘉 宾：因为我想让你们学学新疆食品的做法呀。

Wǒ xiǎng ràng nǐmen xuéxue Xīnjiāng shípǐn de zuòfǎ.
我 想 让 你们 学学 新疆 食品 的 做法。

I want you to learn how to make some traditional Xinjiang cuisine.

大 牛：学做饭啊？这个我在行啊。好，今天我们就来一个自力更生，自给自足。

韩 佳：哎，注意了，注意了啊！“给”是个多音字，在这个成语中我们应该念“jǐ”。自给自足。意思就是说靠自己的生产来满足自己的需求。

大 牛：“自给自足”*这个成语，就是说靠自己的生产来满足自己的需求。*自给自足。好，我宣布开工！

Daniel: Why just ingredients?

Guest: It's because I want you to learn to make some traditional Xinjiang cuisine.

Daniel: Learning to cook? I am good at that. Okay, let's all cook independently and "zi gei zi zu".

Han Jia: Hey, attention, please. The word "gei" is a polyphone. In this idiom, it is pronounced "ji", third tone. "Zi ji zi zu" means "to rely on one's own effort to provide for oneself".

Daniel: "Zi ji zi zu" is a Chinese phrase, which means "to provide independently for oneself". Okay, let's start to work.

场景 Scene 院子外

大　牛：师傅说了，这羊肉串要不停地翻烤，让它们受热均匀。

嘉　宾：好了，现在可以放盐、辣椒、胡椒粉和辣椒粉。

大　牛：好，这个我来③。

嘉　宾：哎呀，你呀还是来尝尝这个吧。

大　牛：好，这个我最擅长。

韩　佳：哎，你怎么就吃上了啊④？

大　牛：没有，没有。烤着呢，烤着呢。韩佳，这个羊肉串看着就香。来，尝一串。

韩　佳：嗯，真香啊！这是你烤的吗？

大　牛：是啊。

韩　佳：哎，对了，不知道大家注意了没有，"串"字用法非常多。

大　牛：对，对，对。比如一串羊肉串。第一个"串"字是量词；一串珍珠，一串糖葫芦。第二个"串"字是名词，羊肉串。

韩　佳：嗯，没错儿。"串"还可以当动词，串门。比如说我们到维吾尔族朋友家来串门。

Wǒmen dào Wéiwú'ěrzú péngyou jiā lái chuàn mén.
我们 到 维吾尔族 朋友 家来 串 门。

We're dropping in on our Uygur friends.

Daniel: Our teacher said the shish-kebabs should be turned repeatedly to let them get heated evenly.

Guest: Now you can scatter some salt, chilli, pepper and chili powder over them.

Daniel: Okay, I can handle this.

Guest: Oh, you'd better taste this first.

Daniel: Okay, that's what I'm most skilled in.

Han Jia: Eh, you've started eating?

Daniel: No, no. I am still roasting the shish-kebabs. Han Jia, the kebabs smell so good. Come on, taste a stick of kebabs.

Han Jia: Oh, it's so delicious! Did you roast them?

Daniel: Yeah.

Han Jia: Oh, yes, have you noticed that the word "chuan" has many usages?

Daniel: Yes, indeed. For instance "yi chuan yangrouchuan" (one stick of lamb kebabs). The first "chuan" is a measure word, as in "yi chuan" (one string of) pearls and "yi chuan" (one stick of) sugarcoated haws. The second "chuan" is a noun as in "yangrouchuan".

Han Jia: Yes, exactly. "Chuan" can also be used as a verb, as in "chuan men" (visit someone). We can say we're dropping in on our Uygur friends.

场景 Scene 室内

韩　佳：这新疆的美食真是风味独特，好吃极了[5]！

大　牛：在今天的节目里，我们还学了一些新疆美食的做法。真是不虚此行[6]！

韩　佳：我们倒是吃了不少，那电视机前的观众朋友们呢？

大　牛：没关系。我相信电视机前的观众朋友们，看了我们今天的节目以后，一定会考虑来新疆品尝的。下面一起进入我们今天的"赏心悦目"，选一选您喜欢的美味吧。

Han Jia: Xinjiang has various kinds of savory food and is all delectable.

Daniel: In today's program, we've also learned to cook a few kinds of Xinjang food. It's really a most rewarding trip.

Han Jia: We two have eaten a lot. What about our viewers?

Daniel: It doesn't matter. I am sure our viewers, after seeing today's program, will consider visiting Xinjiang to taste the food here. Next let's move on to today's *Enjoyable Scenery* to see which food you like best.

生 词 Words and Expressions

1. 英俊	（形）	yīngjùn	handsome
2. 潇洒	（形）	xiāosǎ	natural and unrestrained
3. 民居	（名）	mínjū	dwelling
4. 象征	（动、名）	xiàngzhēng	to symbolize, signify; symbol, emblem
5. 自力更生		zì lì gēng shēng	to provide independently for oneself; self-reliance
6. 均匀	（形）	jūnyún	even
7. 擅长	（动）	shàncháng	to be good at; be expert in
8. 珍珠	（名）	zhēnzhū	pearl
9. 串门	（动）	chuàn mén	to call at sb.'s home; drop in
10. 风味	（名）	fēngwèi	special flavor; local color

注 释 Notes

1. 我们维吾尔族小伙子，除了热情好客以外，还特别英俊潇洒。

“除了……以外，还……”，这一结构表示“还”引出的事物是对前面提到的事物的一种补充，两者是加合关系。

The construction “除了……以外，还……” indicates that in addition to something, there exists something else.

例如：这次报名参加学校游泳比赛的，我们班除了我以外，还有两个人。

2. 民以食为天。

“以……为……”，这一结构相当于“把……作为……”“认为……是……”。

The construction “以……为……”, equivalent to “把……作为……” or “认为……是……”. It means “to take…as…; regard…as…”.

例如：这个地区的经济以农业为主。

“民以食为天”的意思是“人民把吃做看做是生存的依赖”。语出《汉书·郦食其传》，原句为“王者以民为天，而民以食为天。”

“民以食为天” means “the masses regard food as their prime want”. The expression comes from the *Biography of Li Yiji* in *Records of the Historian*.

3. 好，这个我来。

“来”这里代替意义更具体的动词，表示做某个动作。

The verb “来” is used as a substitute for some other verb with a more specific meaning.

例如：这个箱子你搬不动，我来。

4. 你怎么就吃上了啊？

“上”，这里用在动词后表示动作有了结果并兼有达到某种目的意思。

“上” is used after a verb to indicate that an action has got its result and achieved some objective concurrently.

例如：我终于住上新房了。

5. 这新疆的美食真是风味独特，好吃极了！

“形容词／动词＋极了”，这一结构表示最高程度，常用于口语。

The construction “adjective/verb + 极了”, often used in oral Chinese, means “to the greatest extent; extremely; exceedingly”.

例如：这次篮球比赛棒极了。

老师对我们这次考试成绩满意极了。

6. 真是不虚此行！

这里“虚”的意思是白白地、没有效果。“不虚此行”意思是这次到这儿来，很有收获，没有白来。

“虚” here means “in vain”. “不虚此行” means “to take a journey like this is a rewarding one”.

替换练习 Substitution Drills

1. 在	新疆，	几乎每家的	院子	里	都有	葡萄架。
	北京		阳台	上		鲜花
	江南		房子	后		竹林
	农村		房门	前		树

2. 我想让你们	学学	新疆	食品	的	做法。
	看看	北京	烤鸭		烤法
	试试	电子	玩具		玩法
	瞧瞧	泰国	榴莲		吃法

3. 我们到	维吾尔族	朋友家	串门。
	藏族		拜访
	蒙古族		做客
	回族		聚会

会 话 Conversations

完成下列会话 Complete the following dialogues

(如括号里有词语或提示，请按要求做 Use the words or expressions given in the brackets)

A: 新疆的葡萄真多啊！

B: ______________________________。(葡萄架)

A: 新疆还有什么好吃的？

B: ______________________________。(除了……以外，还有……)

A: 你喜欢新疆的烤羊肉串吗？

B: ______________________________。(极了)

A: 这次来新疆没有白来吧？

B: ______________________________。(不虚此行)

维吾尔族民居（二）

【第二十集】

场景 Scene 维吾尔族民居外

大　牛：大家好，欢迎来到《快乐中国》。今天，快乐的韩佳、大牛再带您到维族朋友的家里坐一坐①。

合：快乐学汉语，轻松亚克西！

韩　佳：哎，你怎么说上维吾尔族语了！

大　牛：那是，入乡随俗嘛。大家都知道“亚克西”是好的意思。

韩　佳：嗯，说得倒没错。

嘉　宾：亚克西木塞斯！

大　牛：亚克西……哎，亚克西什么啊？

韩　佳：听不懂了吧？她是在向你问好。“亚克西木塞斯”就是您好的意思。

大　牛：哦，亚克西木塞斯。

韩　佳：这回就对了。虽然我们是客人，但还是要请长者先行。

大　牛：请！

Suīrán wǒmen shì kèrén, dàn háishi yào
虽然 我们 是 客人，但 还是 要
qǐng zhǎngzhě xiān xíng.
请 长者 先 行。

Despite being guests, we ask our senior to go first.

Daniel: Hello, welcome to *Happy China*. Today, happy Han Jia and Daniel will take you to continue our visit to some Uygur friends' homes.

Together: While learning Chinese in a joyful and relaxed and "yakshi" manner.

Han Jia: Hey, you are beginning to speak the Uygur language!

Daniel: When in Rome, do as the Romans do. Everyone knows "yakshi" means good.

Han Jia: Yeah, you're right.

Guest: Yakshimses!

Daniel: Yakshi... Oh, yakshi what?

Han Jia: Don't you understand she says: "How are you?" "Yakshimses" means "how are you?"

Daniel: Oh, yakshimses.

Han Jia: You're right this time. Despite being guests, we ask our senior to go first.

Daniel: Please.

场景 Scene 院子里

韩　佳：哎呀，您家可是典型的维族民居啊。太漂亮了！

嘉　宾：韩佳，你对我们维吾尔族民居了解得真不少。

韩　佳：哪里，哪里②。只是知道一些皮毛。

大　牛：你知道皮毛有什么用？人家问的是维族民居。

韩　佳：我用的是比喻义。皮毛呢，是用来比喻表面的知识。

大　牛：皮毛，*读二声，比喻表面的知识。例如*，我只知道一些皮毛。皮毛。要说我对新疆民居的了解，那可不只是略知皮毛了③。

嘉　宾：哦，大牛，那说说看吧！

大　牛：这维族民居啊早先是吸收了西亚、甘肃和陕西的建筑风格，近代又吸收了俄罗斯的民居艺术。要说它的形状嘛，有一字型、T型，还有凹字型的。您的这个房子是典型的T型啊。

Zhè zuò fángzi shì diǎnxíng de T xíng.

这 座 房子 是 典型 的 T 型。

This house is in the typical T shape.

嘉　宾：不错，不错。没想到你这么了解。请进，请进。

大　牛：谢谢，谢谢。

韩　佳：我的。还给我。

Han Jia: Wow, yours is a typical Uygur dwelling. It's so nice!

Guest: Han Jia, you know quite a lot about our Uygur houses.

Han Jia: Oh, not really. I only know some "pimao".

Daniel: It's no use knowing some"pimao"(skin and fur). He talks about Uygur houses.

Han Jia: I used it as a metaphor. "Pimao" refers to superficial knowledge.

Daniel: "Pimao", two second tones, literally skin and fur, is a metaphor for superficial knowledge. For example, I only know a little bit about it. As for Xinjiang residential houses, I know quite a lot about them.

Guest: Oh, Daniel, tell us what you know.

Daniel: Uygur people first adopted Western Asian, Gansu and Shaanxi architectural styles and later, in modern times, Russian styles. And as for their shapes, there are the flat-roof shape, the T shape and the concave shape. Your house is in the typical T shape.

Guest: You are right. I didn't expect you know so much. Please come in.

Daniel: Thanks.

Han Jia: That's mine. Give it back to me.

场景 Scene　室内

大　牛：韩佳，你看，维吾尔族的茶壶做得多精美啊！我猜是银子做的。

韩　佳：嘘！这是洗手壶。倒出来的水啊是给你洗手的。

大　牛：不好意思。您瞧啊，屋里布置得多精美啊！

韩　佳：是啊。

嘉　宾：大牛，你对维吾尔族建筑外形很了解。它有什么特点？比如说里面的陈设。

大　牛：哦，这个啊……这里面的陈设嘛……韩佳，陈设指的是什么？

韩　佳：就是指屋里摆放的东西。

大　牛：哦，这方面的东西，还是韩佳比较了解。

韩　佳：啊，我觉得啊维族民居最吸引人的是它的色彩。

Wéizú mínjū zuì xīyǐn rén de shì tā de sècǎi.
维族 民居 最 吸引 人 的 是 它 的 色彩。

The most attractive aspect of Uygur dwellings is their color.

大　牛：色彩之外，造型也很有特点④。您瞧，这墙面的刻花和装饰，一般都是花草图案的。

韩　佳：嗯，再加上屋里挂毯和地毯的点缀啊，就更具有维族风情了。

嘉　宾：哎呀，大牛，小韩，真没想到你们这么年轻，对我们民族建筑这么了解！

大　牛：哪里，哪里⑤。

韩　佳：过奖，过奖⑤。哎，外面……

嘉　宾：走，我们出去看看外面的民间舞蹈吧。

大　牛：好！

Daniel: Han Jia, look. How beautifully the teapot is crafted! I guess it's made of silver.

Han Jia: Sh! This is a hand-washing pot. The water poured from it is used for washing your hands.

Daniel: I'm sorry. Look, what a beautifully decorated house!

Han Jia: Yes, indeed.

Guest: Daniel, you are quite knowledgeable about the shapes of Uygur houses. What features do you find in this house's interior furnishings?

Daniel: Oh, about this...the interior "chenshe"...uh, Han Jia, what does "chenshe" refer to?

Han Jia: It refers to interior furnishings.

Daniel: Oh, interior furnishings. Han Jia knows a lot more than I do.

Han Jia: Ah, I think the most attractive aspect of Uygur dwellings is their colors.

Daniel: In addition to colors, the shapes are also very special. Look, the carved patterns on the walls mostly take the shape of flowers and plants.

Han Jia: Yeah, what's more, the decorative tapestries and carpets add more to the ethnic Uygur style.

Guest: Wow, Daniel and Han Jia, we didn't expect you, at such young ages, know so much about our ethnic architecture!

Daniel: Thank you, we are flattered.

Han Jia: I'll take that as a compliment! Oh, outside...

Guest: Let's go outside and see the Uygur folk dance.

Daniel: Good.

场景 Scene 院子里

大　牛：哎呀，跳着这么欢快的舞蹈啊，我真是什么烦心的事儿都没有了。

韩　佳：是啊，我们在这里跳得热火朝天，也应该让电视机前的观众朋友们享受一下了。

大　牛：哎呀，我猜电视机前的观众朋友们早就随着音乐的节拍和我们一起舞蹈了。

韩　佳：来来来，休息一下，一起让我们进入今天的“赏心悦目”。

Daniel: Wow, what a lively dance! All the worries on my mind are gone.

Han Jia: Indeed. While we're dancing here so happily, we should also let our audience have a good time.

Daniel: Hey, I guess our viewers are already dancing with us to the rhythm of the music.

Han Jia: Come on. Let's take a break and together enter today's *Enjoyable Scenery*.

生 词 Words and Expressions

1.	入乡随俗		rù xiāng suí sú	wherever you are, follow the local customs; when in Rome, do as the Romans do
2.	长者	（名）	zhǎngzhě	elder; senior
3.	吸收	（动）	xīshōu	to absorb; draw
4.	布置	（动）	bùzhì	to fix up; arrange; decorate
5.	造型	（名）	zàoxíng	model; mould
6.	装饰	（动、名）	zhuāngshì	to decorate, adorn; decoration, ornament
7.	风情	（名）	fēngqíng	local conditions and customs
8.	烦心	（形）	fánxīn	annoying; vexatious; troublesome
9.	热火朝天		rè huǒ cháo tiān	buzzing with activity; enthusiastically
10.	享受	（动）	xiǎngshòu	to enjoy

注 释 Notes

1. 带您到维吾尔族朋友的家里坐一坐。

“一”放在两个重叠的单音节动词之间，表示行为不很费力或经历时间短，一般多用于尚未发生的或者经常性的动作。

“一” is placed between two repeated monosyllabic verbs to indicate that an action is not difficult or lasts a short time. It is mostly used to express an action that is going to happen or happens at a regular basis.

例如：咱们一起聊一聊吧。

2. 哪里，哪里。

哪里，哪里：这是一种客气的说法，表示否定，单独用在答话里。“哪里”可以单用，也可以两个连用。

“哪里，哪里” or “哪里” is used by itself as a polite reply to a compliment to denote negation.

例如：A：这给你增加麻烦了。

B：哪里，哪里，这是应该做的。

3. 要说我对新疆民居的了解，那可不只是略知皮毛了。

“要说……那（就）……”，这个结构用在假设复句中，在前半句提出一个假设，后半句作出判断或说明。

The construction “要说……那（就）……” is used in an assumptive compound sentence. The former part gives an assumption and in the latter part, a judgement or explanation is made.

例如：要说这件衣服的款式好不好，那就看你的喜好了。

4. 色彩之外，造型也很有特点。

“之外”，指超出一定界限。不能单用。用法与“以外”基本相同，多用于书面语。

“之外”，meaning “besides”，is often used in written Chinese and cannot be used by itself. Its usage is basically the same as that of “以外”。

例如：学习外语，发音之外，语法同样重要。

5. 过奖，过奖。

“过奖”，谦辞，意思是过分地表扬或夸奖，用在别人赞扬自己时。

The self-depreciatory expression “过奖”, meaning “to overpraise; give undeserved compliment”, is used as a polite reply to a compliment.

例如：您过奖了，我的英语水平只是一般。

替换练习 Substitution Drills

1. 虽然我们是 客人， 但还是要请 长者 先 行。

客人	长者	先	行
外国人	老师		吃
同行	来宾		发言
熟人	女士		上车

2. 这座 房子 是典型的 T 型。

房子	T
大楼	工字
展览馆	凹字
建筑	丁字

3. 维吾尔族 民居 最吸引人的是它的 色彩。

维吾尔族	民居	色彩
基督	教堂	尖顶
佛教	寺庙	大屋顶
江南	住宅	青瓦白墙

会 话 Conversations

完成下列会话 Complete the following dialogues

（如括号里有词语或提示，请按要求做 Use the words or expressions given in the brackets）

A: 维吾尔族的房屋造型真有特点啊！

B: ________________________________。（……一……）

A: 好啊，进去吧。

B: ________________________________。（布置）

A: 你们房子装饰得真漂亮！

B: ________________________________。（哪里）

A: 真的，比城里的房子还要干净、漂亮。

B: ________________________________。（过奖）

中哈边界——霍尔果斯口岸

【第二十二集】

场景 Scene　中哈边界界碑旁

韩　佳：大牛，节目一开始怎么就做起体操来了①？

大　牛：谁做体操了？

韩　佳：那你就是在冒充稻草人？

大　牛：韩佳，麦田离这里还有好几公里啊，我没事冒充稻草人干吗？你得深入地看问题啊！

韩　佳：哦！

大　牛：知道了？

韩　佳：知道了。你又在故弄玄虚②。

大　牛：我告诉你啊，我的这个动作可是有深刻含义的。现在我的右手是在中国的境内，而我的左手呢可是在哈萨克斯坦的境内。这里就是中哈两国的边界，以界碑为证。

韩　佳：你以为界碑就是边界啊？界碑只是一种标识，并不是真正的边界。

大　牛：有什么不同吗？

韩　佳：当然不同了。界标和边界可是两个概念。

Jièbiāo hé biānjiè kě shì liǎng ge gàiniàn.
界标 和 边界 可 是 两 个 概念。

Boundary markers and borderlines are two different concepts.

Han Jia: Daniel, why are you doing exercise at the beginning of our program?

Daniel: I'm not doing exercise at all.

Han Jia: Are you pretending to be a scarecrow?

Daniel: Han Jia, the wheat fields are miles away from here. Why should I pretend to be a scarecrow here? You should look at things from a deeper perspective.

Han Jia: Huh!

Daniel: Now understand?

Han Jia: I understand it's a fuss about nothing again.

Daniel: Let me tell you. My posture like this means a great deal. My right hand is inside the Chinese territory while my left hand in the territory of Kazakhstan. This is the border between China and Kazakhstan, as proved by this boundary marker.

Han Jia: You thought the boundary marker means the borderline? A boundary marker is only a symbol, not the exact borderline.

Daniel: Are there any differences?

Han Jia: Of course there are. Boundary markers and borderlines are two different concepts.

韩　佳：边界是两国法律上的分界，而界标呢是起到标识分界作用的标志。

大　牛：啊，不早说啊？刚才两只胳膊举了半天，酸死了[3]。那真正的边界在哪儿啊？

韩　佳：真正的中哈边界啊，就是我们身后的这条霍尔果斯河。以航道的中心为界，那边就是哈萨克斯坦的境内了。

大　牛：这我得好好看看。

场景 Scene　中哈边界线

韩　佳：哎，大牛，你可不能再往前走了。

大　牛：怎么了？不是还没过桥呢吗？

韩　佳：你可千万不能往前走了[4]！看看脚底下的桥面有什么不同。

大　牛：哦，对。这路面两边的颜色不一样啊！

韩　佳：对啊。这座桥叫霍尔果斯桥。桥的正中间也正好是界河的航道中心。所以呢……

大　牛：所以路面偏白的这一面是中国，偏黑的那一面就是哈萨克斯坦[5]。

韩　佳：嗯，没错儿。你可要小心，不要越界哟！

大　牛：哎呀，异国风情就在我眼前啊！我望……我望……我望而却步啊！

韩　佳：嘿，知道的成语还不少，就是用得不是地方。

大　牛：啊？

韩　佳：“望而却步”的“却”是后退的意思。“望而却步”这个成语是指遇到了危险或者是做不到的事情，就往后退缩了。望而却步。

大　牛：嗯，的确用得不是地方。看不到异国风情有一点儿遗憾啊！

Han Jia: A borderline is the legal demarcation between two countries. And a boundary marker serves as a symbol of the demarcation line.

Daniel: Hey, why didn't you say this earlier? I held up my arms for a long time and now they are sore. Then where is the exact borderline?

Han Jia: The exact Sino-Kazak borderline is the Horgos River behind us, with the middle of the water course as the demarcation line. That side is the territory of Kazakhstan.

Daniel: Let me take a close look.

Han Jia: Hey, Daniel, you can't go further ahead.

Daniel: Why not? I haven't crossed the bridge yet.

Han Jia: You mustn't go forward any further! Look if there is anything different on the bridge surface.

Daniel: Okay. The two parts of the surface are different in color.

Han Jia: Yes. This bridge is called the Horgos Bridge. Its middle is this river's central line. So...

Daniel: So, the part in white is Chinese and the darker part is Kazakhstan.

Han Jia: Yes, exactly. You must be careful not to cross the boundary.

Daniel: Wow, the land of a foreign country is right before me. But I have to "wang er que bu".

Han Jia: Hey, you know so many idioms. But it's not aptly used.

Daniel: Really?

Han Jia: The "que" in "wang er que bu" means "to shrink back". The idiom "wang er que bu" means "to shrink back at the sight of something dangerous or difficult". "Wang er que bu".

Daniel: Yes, I did use it inappropriately. It is a pity not to be able to see the foreign lifestyle.

韩　佳：别遗憾啊。不过去并不代表看不到啊⑥！
大　牛：什么意思？
韩　佳：你忘了啊，这里自古以来边境贸易就十分繁荣。

Zhèli zì gǔ yǐlái biānjìng màoyì jiù shífēn fánróng.
这里 自 古 以来 边境 贸易 就 十分 繁荣。
Trade along the border here has been flourishing since ancient times.

韩　佳：离这儿不远呢，就是有名的中哈一条街。我们可以去那边看看。
大　牛：*逛商场？走！*

场景 Scene　霍尔果斯口岸中哈商品街

韩　佳：您看，这里卖的都是伊犁当地的工艺品，还有很多哈萨克斯坦的商品。瞧瞧，这披肩多漂亮啊！很有特色。
大　牛：小姐，好眼光啊！
韩　佳：大牛，你在这儿干什么呢？
大　牛：我叫穆罕穆德·买买提·大牛。你可以叫我买买提。
韩　佳：行了，行了，别捣乱了！赶快把老板给我叫出来。
大　牛：这不是在这儿呢吗？
韩　佳：啊？你想干吗？
大　牛：我想……我想向您推荐这把小刀。
韩　佳：吓我一跳⑦！
大　牛：这叫英吉沙小刀，是新疆四大名刀之一，绝对物超所值。

Han Jia: I don't think it's that much of a pity. Being unable to cross the bridge doesn't mean you cannot see the sight.

Daniel: What do you mean?

Han Jia: Don't you know that trade along the border here has been flourishing since ancient times?

Han Jia: Not far from here, there is a street called Sino-Kazak Street. We can go over and have a look.

Daniel: Shopping? Let's go.

Han Jia: You see, this place sells mostly local Ili handicraft products, as well as goods from Kazakhstan. Look, how pretty this cape is! Very special.

Daniel: Miss, you have an eye for nice things.

Han Jia: Daniel, what are you doing here?

Daniel: My name is Muhammad Maimaiti Daniel. Or just call me Maimaiti.

Han Jia: Hey, no more pranks! Call out the owner of this stall.

Daniel: Here he is.

Han Jia: What? What do you want to do?

Daniel: I want... I want to recommend this small knife to you.

Han Jia: I was startled.

Daniel: This is called Yengisar Knife, one of the most famous four knives in Xinjiang. It's absolutely "wu chao suo zhi".

韩　佳：真的吗？

大　牛：对呀。“物超所值”*就是说货物的质量超出了价格*。物超所值。例如，这把精致的小刀绝对物超所值。

Zhè bǎ jīngzhì de xiǎo dāo juéduì wù chāo suǒ zhí.
这把精致的小刀绝对物超所值。

This exquisite little knife is worth more than it’s being sold for.

韩　佳：是吗？那谢谢了啊。别忘了付钱。

大　牛：哎，韩佳，我没带钱。

嘉　宾：老板，这刀多少钱？

　　合：小姐，好眼光。

大　牛：哎，韩佳，我发现冒充店铺老板的不止我一个啊[8]！

韩　佳：不过啊，咱俩都不像。还是干咱俩的老本行吧[9]。看看今天的“赏心悦目”！

Han Jia: Really?

Daniel: Yes. "Wu chao suo zhi" means something is worth more than it actually costs. For example, this exquisite knife is surely "wu chao suo zhi".

Han Jia: Really? Thanks a lot. Don't forget to pay for it.

Daniel: Oh, Han Jia, I forgot to bring money with me.

Guest: Excuse me. How much is this knife?

Together: Miss, you have an eye.

Daniel: Hey, Han Jia, I found I wasn't the only one pretending to be the owner of this stall.

Han Jia: But, I think neither of us is like a businessman. We'd better go about our own business. Please watch today's *Enjoyable Scenery*.

生 词 Words and Expressions

1. 冒充	（动）	màochōng	to pretend to be; pass off as
2. 含义	（名）	hányì	meaning; implication
3. 标识	（名）	biāozhì	sign; mark; symbol
4. 航道	（名）	hángdào	channel; sea-lane; course
5. 异国风情		yìguó fēngqíng	exotic conditions and customs
6. 退缩	（动）	tuìsuō	to shrink back; flinch; cower
7. 繁荣	（形）	fánróng	flourishing; prosperous; booming
8. 披肩	（名）	pījiān	cape
9. 推荐	（动）	tuījiàn	to recommend
10. 精致	（形）	jīngzhì	fine; exquisite; delicate

注 释 Notes

1. 节目一开始怎么就做起体操来了？

“一……就……”，这一结构表示一个动作或情况出现后紧接着发生另一个动作或情况，可以是一个主语，也可以分属两个主语。

The construction “一……就……” indicates that once an action happens, another one will happen immediately after it. And it may have one or two subjects.

例如：他每天下班回来，一进门就打开电视。

我一到车站，汽车就来了。

2. 你又在故弄玄虚。

故弄玄虚是指故意玩弄使人迷惑的欺骗手段。

“故弄玄虚” means “to purposely make a mystery of simple things; deliberately mystifying”.

例如：你这是故弄玄虚，我们才不相信呢。

3. 刚才两只胳膊举了半天，酸死了。

这里“半天”指相当长的一段时间。

“半天” refers to a rather long period of time.

例如：你上哪儿了？我等你半天了。

“死”，在这里是形容词。用在某些动词或形容词后，表示达到极点。句尾多带助词“了”。

“死” here is an adjective, meaning “extremely; to death”. It is used after some verbs or adjectives and is often followed by the particle “了”.

例如：这几天我忙死了，一点儿休息时间也没有。

4. 你可千万不能往前走了！

“千万”，副词，表示恳切叮咛，“必须”“一定要”的意思。

The adverb “千万” means “to be sure to; must”.

例如：刚才跟你说的事，你千万不要忘记了。

5. 所以路面偏白的这一面是中国，偏黑的那一面就是哈萨克斯坦。

“偏”，这里是动词，表示偏重，比较。

The verb “偏” means “to incline to one side; slant; lean”.

例如：这根柱子栽歪了，有点儿偏左，向右一点儿就行了。

6. 不过去并不代表看不到啊！

“并”，副词，加强否定的语气，放在“不”“没（有）”前边。常用在表示转折的句子中，有否定某种看法、说明真实情况的意味。

The adverb “并” is used before “不” or “没（有）” to intensify the tone of negation. It is often used in transitional sentences, indicating the negation of some opinion and explanation of the truth.

例如：那件事，他并没有告诉我，所以我也不知道怎么办。

7. 吓我一跳！

在这句话中，“我”是动词“吓”的宾语，“一跳”是“吓”的补语，表示害怕的情态。这种同时带有宾语和补语的动词谓语句，补语要放在宾语后。

In this sentence, “我” is the object of the verb “吓”, and “一跳” is the complement of “吓”, indicating astonishment. In such a sentence with a verb predicate containing both an object and a complement, the complement should be placed after the object.

例如：昨天爸爸骂了我一顿。

8. 我发现冒充店铺老板的不止我一个啊!

"不止"，动词，表示超出一定的数量。

The verb "不止" means "to exceed a certain amount".

例如：我们班喜欢游泳的人不止十个吧?

9. 还是干咱俩的老本行吧。

"本行"，是指一贯从事的或长期已经熟习的行业。"老本行"更强调从事某一行业时间长，特别熟习。

"本行" refers to the profession that one has been consistently engaged in or familiar with. "老本行" emphasizes that the period of time one has been engaged in some profession is quite long or one is rather familiar with his job.

例如：教书是我的老本行。

替换练习 Substitution Drills

1.	界标	和	边界	可是两	个	概念。
	熊猫		树熊		种	动物
	荔枝		龙眼		类	水果
	大连		大理		座	城市

2.	这里自古以来	边界	贸易	就十分	繁荣。
		水陆	交通		便利
		丝绸	产业		发达
		各种	水果		有名

3.	这	把	精致	的	小刀	绝对物超所值。
		件	漂亮		毛衣	
		台	新款		电脑	
		座	临海		别墅	

会 话 Conversations

完成下列会话 Complete the following dialogues
（如括号里有词语或提示，请按要求做 Use the words or expressions given in the brackets）

A: 你是做什么工作的？
B: ________________________________。（老本行）
A: 我和你一样，也是教师。
B: ________________________________。（……半天）

A: 你想去逛逛露天市场吗？
B: ________________________________。（一……就……）
A: 那我们现在就去露天市场吧。
B: ________________________________。（千万）

草原之夜风情园

【第二十二集】

场景 Scene 亭子里

韩　佳：嗬，大牛，几天不见，你欣赏起经典作品来了啊[1]！

大　牛：韩佳，你应该知道，我一向对经典音乐很有研究，尤其是舒伯特的代表作《小夜曲》[2]，真是太美了！

韩　佳：哎，那太巧了！我今天啊，就要说说小夜曲。

大　牛：甭说了，听我唱不就得了嘛[3]。

韩　佳：哎，等会儿，等会儿，大牛。

大　牛：哦，对。《快乐中国》嘛，你要听中文版的。我的歌声穿过黑夜……

韩　佳：哎，行了行了，大牛。我说的是原汁原味的东方“小夜曲”。

Wǒ shuō de shì yuán zhī yuán wèi de
我　说　的　是　原　汁　原　味　的
dōngfāng “Xiǎoyèqǔ”.
东方　“小夜曲”。

I'm talking about the original oriental *Eine Kleine Machtmusik*.

大　牛：东方“小夜曲”啊？

韩　佳：对啊。你听！

大　牛：这么悠扬的歌声太好听了。

韩　佳：这回大牛形容词还用得挺准确，悠扬的歌声。

大　牛：悠扬，*“悠”读一声，“扬”读二声，形容声音时高时低，非常和谐。*悠扬。

韩　佳：嗯，没错儿。“悠扬”这个词啊用来形容声音时高时低，非常和谐。用它来形容动听的歌声啊再合适不过了[4]。

大　牛：韩佳，已经说了半天了。到底是什么歌啊？

韩　佳：急什么？跟我来！

Han Jia: Ha, Daniel, I haven't seen you for a couple of days and now you've turned to be fond of classical music!

Daniel: Han Jia, you ought to know I am well versed in classical music, especially Schubert's representative work, *Eine Kleine Nachtmusik*, which is so beautiful.

Han Jia: As it happens, today we're going to talk about serenades.

Daniel: Don't talk. Just listen to me singing it.

Han Jia: Hey, wait a minute, Daniel.

Daniel: Oh, yeah, yeah. For our program, *Happy China*, you want to listen to the Chinese version, *my song crosses the moonlit night sky*...

Han Jia: Okay, enough. Daniel, I'm talking about the original oriental *Eine Kleine Nachtmusik*.

Daniel: *Eine Kleine Nachtmusik*?

Han Jia: Yeah. Listen!

Daniel: What a "youyang de" song! It's so melodious.

Han Jia: This time, Daniel used his adjective correctly, a "youyang de" song.

Daniel: "Youyang", first tone, second tone, means melodious. "Youyang".

Han Jia: Yes, exactly. The word "youyang" refers to a voice or music rising and falling harmoniously. It is most appropriate to use it to describe a melodious song.

Daniel: Han Jia, you've talked so much. What song is it after all?

Han Jia: Take it easy. Come with me.

场景 Scene 草原之夜风情园

韩　佳：大牛，瞧。这就是刚才的歌声所表现的场景。

大　牛：可克达拉草原之夜，还是“草原小夜曲”啊！

韩　佳：是啊，诞生在草原，描述草原。所以说可克达拉草原是这首歌的诞生地。

大　牛：那第二点描述草原呢？

韩　佳：五十多年前的一个黄昏，张加毅老师和田歌老师，看见人们工作之余躺在草地上放松地唱歌，于是啊，有感而发，很快地就写出了这首歌曲[5]。

Tāmen yǒu gǎn ér fā, hěn kuài jiù xiěchūle
他们 有 感 而 发，很 快 就 写出了
zhè shǒu gēqǔ.
这 首 歌曲。

They were inspired and in no time the song was completed.

大　牛：他们两位真是一气呵成。

韩　佳：“一气呵成”就是说一口气就完成了。现在通常用来比喻写文章、说话非常顺畅，整个工作非常迅速就完成了。

大　牛：“一气呵成”*这个成语，意思是一口气就完成了*。一气呵成。

韩　佳：后来啊，这首歌飘出了草原，被联合国教科文组织命名为“世界东方小夜曲”。

大　牛：这么了不起[6]！我决定了，我的阿肯之路就从《草原之夜》开始[7]。

韩　佳：怎么啊，你要学唱这首歌啊？

大　牛：啊。

韩　佳：哎，不如啊我们也学学演奏？自弹自唱多惬意啊！

大　牛：好主意！

Han Jia: Daniel, look. This is the site described in the song we heard just now.

Daniel: The night on the Kekdala Grassland, also known as the "Grassland Serenade".

Han Jia: Yes, the song was born on the grassland and describes the grassland. So the Kekdala Grassland is the birthplace of this song.

Daniel: Who wrote the song describing the grassland?

Han Jia: One day, at dusk, over 50 years ago, Zhang Jiayi and Tian Ge saw workers lying on the grass and singing leisurely during the break. They were inspired and in no time the song was completed.

Daniel: They really did it "yiqi he cheng".

Han Jia: "Yiqi he cheng" means to complete something in one go. Currently, it is often used to describe a writing or speech which was done very smoothly and quickly.

Daniel: "Yiqi he cheng" is a Chinese idiom, which means to complete something all in one go.

Han Jia: Later, this song spread beyond the grassland and was designated by UNESCO as the "*World's Oriental Serenade*".

Daniel: It's amazing. I've decided to follow the Akens' example and start from the *Night on the Grassland*.

Han Jia: What? Do you want to learn this song?

Daniel: Yes.

Han Jia: Eh, wouldn't it be better for us to learn to play their instruments as well? It'd be cool to sing and play simultaneously!

Daniel: Good idea!

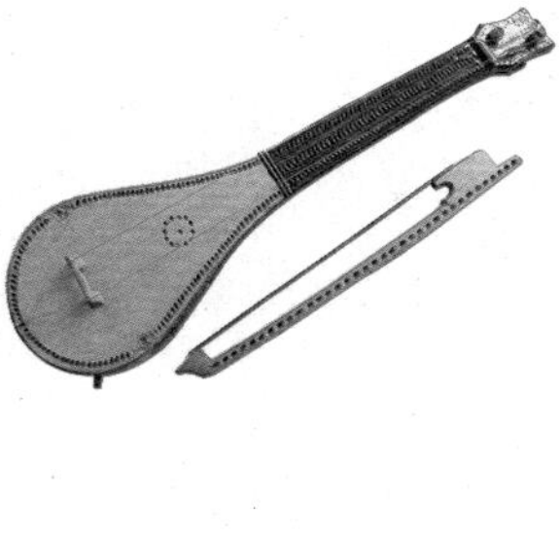

场景 Scene 草原

韩　佳：主意倒是不错，不过做起来就不那么容易了。我俩啊得先找到新疆的特色乐器再说。

大　牛：甭找啦，我来啦！韩佳，你觉得我学哪一种好啊？

韩　佳：我觉得你应该先接受普及教育。

大　牛：怎么了啊？

韩　佳：你拿的这俩啊都是最具有代表性的哈萨克族乐器——冬不拉。

大　牛：啊，都是冬不拉？

韩　佳：对啊。冬不拉的音箱有两种样子。你看，这种呢，叫阿巴衣冬不拉，你那种叫江布尔冬不拉。两种冬不拉外形不同，音色也各有千秋。

Liǎng zhǒng dōngbùlā wàixíng bù tóng, yīnsè yě
两　种　冬不拉　外形　不　同，音色　也

gè yǒu qiān qiū.
各　有　千　秋。

The two Tamboura are different in shape, each having its own characteristic sound.

场景 Scene 草原

合：草原上只留下我的琴声。

韩　佳：嗯，这夕阳西下，大草原真是太美了！

大　牛：别光顾着看美景啊，赶紧练琴。您倒是可以看看美景啊，等我们练好了您再回来。

Han Jia: It is a good idea, but it is not an easy job to learn. We two have to find typical Xinjiang musical instruments in the first place.

Daniel: You don't have to. Here you are. Han Jia, which instrument should I learn to play first?

Han Jia: I think you should receive some basic education first.

Daniel: Why?

Han Jia: The two instruments you are holding are both the most typical Kazak musical instrument—Tamboura.

Daniel: What, they are both Tamboura?

Han Jia: Yeah. There are two kinds of sound boxes. You see, with this kind, it's called *Abayi* Tamboura. What is that kind? That's called *Jangbu'er* Tamboura. The two Tamboura are different in shape, each having its own characteristic sound.

Together: "On the prairie, only the sound of my music lingers on."

Han Jia: Oh, under the sunset glow, the grassland is so beautiful!

Daniel: Don't get distracted by the scenery. We will concentrate on our practice, while you can enjoy the scenery. You'll be back after we learn the skill.

生 词 Words and Expressions

1. 原汁原味		yuán zhī yuán wèi	authentic; original
2. 悠扬	（形）	yōuyáng	rising and falling; melodious; melodic
3. 和谐	（形）	héxié	harmonious
4. 场景	（名）	chǎngjǐng	scene
5. 诞生	（动）	dànshēng	to be born; come into being; emerge
6. 描述	（动）	miáoshù	to describe
7. 黄昏	（名）	huánghūn	dusk
8. 顺畅	（形）	shùnchàng	smooth and easy; unhindered
9. 千秋	（名）	qiānqiū	(each has) its own merits
10. 夕阳西下		xīyáng xī xià	the sun is setting in the west

注 释 Notes

1. 你欣赏起经典作品来了啊！

“起来”，是动词“欣赏”的趋向补语，表示动作的发生。动词的宾语要放在“起”和“来”中间。

“起来” acts as the complement of direction of the verb “欣赏”, indicating that an action happens. The object of the verb should be placed between “起” and “来”.

例如：他也喝起酒来了。

2. 我一向对经典音乐很有研究，尤其是舒伯特的代表作《小夜曲》。

“尤其”，副词，表示在全体中或与其他事物比较时特别突出。一般用在句子的后一部分。

The adverb “尤其”, generally appearing in the latter part of a sentence, indicates that something is very prominent in the whole or as compared with other things.

例如：北京的风沙比较多，尤其是春天。

3. 甭说了，听我唱不就得了嘛。

“甭”，“不用”的合音词。用于口语，这里表示不需要。

The colloquial expression “甭”, the synaeresis of “不用”, means “don’t; needn’t”.

例如：这件事我已经知道了，你甭说了。

“得了”，动词，意思是算了，这里略有不满的意味。

The verb “得了” means “to let it go; forget it” and contains the tone of dissatisfaction somehow.

例如：既然是你不对，那你给他道个歉不就得了。

4. 用它来形容动听的歌声啊再合适不过了。

“不过”，放在由程度副词修饰形容词的偏正结构之后，表示一种程度的极限。意思是再怎么样也不会超过。

“不过” is used after a structure consisting a degree adverb and the adjective it modifies to show the limit of degree, meaning “cannot be more”.

例如：这样好的苹果卖一块钱一斤再便宜不过了。

5. 于是啊，有感而发，很快地就写出了这首歌曲。

“于是”，连词，表示后一件事是承接前一件事或是前一件事的结果。

The conjunction “于是” indicates that the latter thing continues from the former or is its result.

例如：小张讲了这次旅游的具体安排，于是我又决定跟大家一起去。

6. 这么了不起！

“了不起”，意思是“突出，超过一般”。

“了不起” means “amazing; terrific; extraordinary”.

例如：他真了不起，一个人能干几个人的活儿。

7. 我的阿肯之路就从《草原之夜》开始。

“从……开始”同“从……起……”，表示开始时间或起点的范围。

The construction “从……开始”, equivalent to “从……起”, indicates the starting time or starting point.

例如：从明天开始学校正式放假。

取消农业税先从部分地区开始。

替换练习 Substitution Drills

1. 我	说	的是原汁原味的	东方“小夜曲”。
	看		京剧
	听		“梁祝”交响乐
	吃		台湾牛肉面

2. 他们有感而发，	很快	就写出了这	首	歌曲。
	一夜		篇	文章
	几天		个	剧本
	半天		段	相声

3. 两种	冬不拉	外形不同，	音色	也各有	千秋。
	汽车	价钱	功能		区别
	药品	成分	疗效		特点
	房子	外观	户型		差异

会 话 Conversations

完成下列会话 Complete the following dialogues

（如括号里有词语或提示，请按要求做 Use the words or expressions given in the brackets）

A: 大牛，进来，我们一起听音乐吧。

B: ______________________________。（听起……来了）

A: 我最喜欢交响乐《梁祝》，你呢？

B: ______________________________。

A: 要听哪一段？

B: ______________________________。（从……开始）

A: 阿炳的《二泉映月》你听过吗？

B: ______________________________。（了不起）

林公渠

【第二十三集】

场景 Scene 林则徐纪念馆外

韩　佳：伟大的民族英雄林则徐[1]，曾经在伊犁的惠远古城居住了两年多。时间虽然不长，但是却留下了很多造福人类的创举。阿齐乌苏渠的龙口工程就是其中的一件。

场景 Scene 林则徐纪念馆内

韩　佳：龙口工程给当地的居民带来了极大的福利，老百姓都叫它林公渠。这就是当时修建林公渠的工地场景。瞧瞧，他们干得多起劲儿啊[2]！

大　牛：韩佳，你可真够慢的！你怎么才来啊？

韩　佳：大牛，怎么是你啊？

大　牛：嗯，是我。我来亲自感受一下工程修建现场的火热气氛。

Wǒ lái gǎnshòu yíxià zhèli de huǒrè qìfēn.
我 来 感受 一下 这里 的 火热 气氛。

I want to experience for myself the fiery atmosphere here.

韩　佳：哎呀，你呀吓我一跳。

大　牛：我才吓了一跳呢！

韩　佳：啊？我又没干什么。

大　牛：我是说我被林则徐修渠的壮举给吓了一跳。

韩　佳：哦，那看来你对这项工程还挺了解。

大　牛：那当然了。今天你就听我给你讲讲吧。

韩　佳：好吧。

Han Jia: The great national hero, Lin Zexu, lived in Huiyuan of Ili for over two years. Although it wasn't a long time, he accomplished a number of deeds that benefit posterity. One of them was the Longkou Project of the Aqiwusu Canal.

Han Jia: The Longkou Project benefited locals so greatly that they named it the Lingong Canal. This shows how the Lingong Canal was built then. Look, how enthusiastically they are working!

Daniel: Han Jia, you are so slow. Why are you late?

Han Jia: Daniel, what a pleasant surprise to see you here!

Daniel: Yeah, it's me. I want to experience for myself the fiery atmosphere here.

Han Jia: Oh, you took me by surprise!

Daniel: It's me who was startled!

Han Jia: What? I didn't do anything unusual.

Daniel: I mean I was startled by Lin Zexu's exploits.

Han Jia: Oh, you seem to know quite well about this project.

Daniel: Of course I do. Today let me explain.

Han Jia: Okay.

场景 Scene　水利工程图示前

大　牛：韩佳，1844年林则徐捐资修建的是喀什河饮水渠最艰巨、最关键的龙口工程。

韩　佳：这个我们都知道。你能不能给我们介绍一下整个工程的具体情况[3]？

大　牛：没问题。大家用了四个月的时间修建了一条六里长的水渠。这条龙口工程修成之后，就贯通了一条从龙口一直到惠远城东二百一十五公里长的大水渠，使得当地十万余亩荒地变成了良田。

韩　佳：嗬，你了解得够清楚的呀！说得真好！

大　牛：总之一句话，林则徐为修建这条渠道作出了卓越的贡献[4]。

韩　佳：嗯，说得没错儿。

Lín Zéxú zhēn shì zuòchūle zhuóyuè de gòngxiàn.
林则徐 真 是 作出了 卓越 的 贡献。

Lin Zexu really made an outstanding constribution.

大　牛：韩佳，这么有名的水利工程，我们是不是应该去实地看一看呢？

韩　佳：好，说走就走[5]！

大　牛：走。

Daniel: Han Jia, in 1844, Lin Zexu funded the construction of the Longkou Project, the most difficult and crucial part of the drinking water canal diverting water from Kashi River.

Han Jia: We all know about this. Can you be more specific about the entire project?

Daniel: No problem. It took them four months to build a 3-kilometer canal. The completion of the Longkou Project marked the opening of a 215-kilometer canal between Longkou and eastern Huiyuan, making over 100,000 *mu* of wasteland into fertile cropland.

Han Jia: Ha, you know it so clearly. Good job.

Daniel: All in all, Lin Zexu made extraordinary contributions to the construction of this canal.

Han Jia: Yes, absolutely.

Daniel: Han Jia, it's a well-known hydropower project. Do you think we should go there for a look?

Han Jia: Good. Let's go.

Daniel: Let's go.

场景 Scene　水渠前

大　牛：咦，怎么像是站在了丁字路口呢[⑥]？三面都是水渠啊！哪条是林则徐修建的呢？

韩　佳：就是……咳，哪条都不是。

大　牛：啊？你开什么玩笑啊？

韩　佳：我没开玩笑。咱们眼前的真的不是林公渠啊。

大　牛：那我接着找。

韩　佳：哎，等等。但是这里跟林公渠可有着千丝万缕的联系。

大　牛：有什么联系？

韩　佳：林公渠在服务了一百二十三年之后，一九六七年就被我们眼前的渠首枢纽工程所取代了。

大　牛：什么，渠首枢纽工程？

韩　佳：喀什河渠首枢纽工程是在林公渠的基础上建造起来的。这项工程可以保证一百六十万亩土地的灌溉。

Daniel: Hey, we seem to be at a T-shaped crossroads. Two canals meet here. Which was the one built by Lin Zexu?

Han Jia: It is... Hey, neither of them.

Daniel: What? You must be kidding.

Han Jia: I am not kidding. Neither of the canals before us is the Lingong Canal.

Daniel: Then let me go on finding it.

Han Jia: Hey, wait a minute. But this place is closely related with the Lingong Canal.

Daniel: Why?

Han Jia: Having been in service for 123 years, the Lingong Canal was replaced in 1967 by this canal head project in front of us.

Daniel: A canal head project?

Han Jia: The Kashi River canal head project was built on the basis of the Lingong Canal. This project can ensure the irrigation of nearly 1,600,000 *mu* of farmland.

大　牛：我明白了。新水渠修好之后，收益地区更广了。

韩　佳：错。

大　牛：怎么了？

韩　佳：别误会。我是说你用词用错了。在这里呢，我们应该用“受益”，而不应该用收益。“收益”是指生产上或者商业上的收入，而“受益”才是指得到好处、得到利益的意思。

大　牛：哦，我明白了。“收益”，*“收”读一声，“益”读四声，指生产上或者商业上的收入。“受益”，读四声，指得到好处，得到利益的意思。*受益。知错就改，我再说一遍。新水渠修好之后，受益地区更广了。

Xīn shuǐqú xiūhǎo hòu, shòuyì dìqū gèng guǎng le.
新水渠修好后，受益地区更广了。

Now that the new irrigation canal has been completed, even more areas benefit from its waters.

韩　佳：这渠首枢纽工程还有一个独特之处呢。

大　牛：还有什么独特之处呢？

韩　佳：想知道啊，那就得……

大　牛：明白了，爬。

Daniel: I see. After the completion of this new canal, more places receive.

Han Jia: Wrong.

Daniel: What's wrong?

Han Jia: Don't get me wrong. I mean you used a wrong word. Here, we should use "shouyi" two 4th tones instead of "shouyi" 1st tone, 4th tone to refer to the income from production or business, while "shouyi" means "to benefit from".

Daniel: Oh, I see. "shouyi", first tone, fourth tone, means "profit" or "income". But "shouyi", two fourth tones, is a verb which means "to benefit from". One should correct his mistake onces awares of it. Now let me say it again. Now that the new irrigation canal has been completed, even more areas benefit from its waters.

Han Jia: There is a unique aspect with the canal head project.

Daniel: What's that?

Han Jia: If you want to find it out, you have to...

Daniel: Got it. I have to climb.

场景 Scene 林公渠上

大　牛：韩佳，我可算是爬上来了⑦。你赶紧说说，这项工程到底独特在哪儿啊？

韩　佳：其实都不用我说。你一看不就明白了吗？这里是利用环岛的弯道，把水引导到另外一个方向去。

大　牛：这样就有更多的地方会被灌溉。

韩　佳：嗯，聪明！说对了。

大　牛：聪明的是枢纽工程的设计者。他们真是独具匠心。佩服佩服。

韩　佳：你呀，别感慨了！我们今天节目结束的时间是不是该到了呀？

大　牛：谁说的？我们还没有看今天的“赏心悦目”呢。

韩　佳：哦，对，对。

Daniel: Han Jia, I've finally climbed on top of it. Tell me now what's unique about this project.

Han Jia: Actually it's needless to say. You can see it for yourself. Through the circular watercourse around the island, water can be diverted into another direction.

Daniel: Thus more farmland can be irrigated.

Han Jia: Yeah, you are smart.

Daniel: The real smart people are the designers of this pivotal project. They did show an inventive mind. I deeply admire them.

Han Jia: Oh, don't be too sentimental. Is it about time for our program to end?

Daniel: No. We haven't watched the *Enjoyable Scenery* yet.

Han Jia: Oh, you are right.

生 词 Words and Expressions

1. 创举	(名)	chuàngjǔ	pioneering work
2. 壮举	(名)	zhuàngjǔ	magnificent feat; heroic undertaking
3. 捐资	(动)	juān zī	to contribute money; donate
4. 贯通	(动)	guàntōng	to link up; thread together
5. 卓越	(形)	zhuóyuè	outstanding; brilliant
6. 贡献	(动、名)	gòngxiàn	to contribute, devote; contribution, dedication
7. 千丝万缕		qiān sī wàn lǚ	countless ties; innumerable links
8. 枢纽	(名)	shūniǔ	pivot; hub; key position
9. 灌溉	(动)	guàngài	to irrigate
10. 独具匠心		dú jù jiàngxīn	to show ingenuity; have originality

注 释 Notes

1. 林则徐

林则徐（1785－1850），清末政治家，为当时禁烟派代表人物。曾受命到广东查禁鸦片输入，屡次打退英军武装挑衅。后任两广总督。鸦片战争后，因受投降派诬害而被撤职，后被充军新疆。

Lin Zexu (1785－1850), a statesman in the last years of the Qing Dynasty, was the head of a group of Chinese court officials who vehemently opposed the influx of opium into China. He was once ordered to go to Guangdong to suppress the influx of opium and repeatedly repulsed the British army' s armed provocation. Later he was appointed Governor-General of Guangdong and Guangxi. After the Opium Wars, framed up by the capitulationists, he was dismissed from his post and then was exiled to Xinjiang.

2. 他们干得多起劲儿啊！

"起劲儿"，表示情绪高，劲头大。多用于口语。

"起劲儿", meaning "vigorous; energetic; enthusiastic", is often used in oral Chinese.

例如：别打扰他，他玩儿得正起劲儿呢。

3. 你能不能给我们介绍一下整个工程的具体情况？

“一下”，“下”是量词，表示动作次数。“一下”放在动词后表示一次短促的动作。

The construction “一下”, in which “下” is a measure word for times, is put after a verb to indicate a transitory action.

例如：让我看一下。

你去问一下他。

4. 总之一句话，林则徐为修建这条渠道作出了卓越的贡献。

“总之”，在这里有“反正”的意思。表示说话人由于某种原因，不能或不愿意说出确切的情况，而只说出大致的事实或结论。

“总之” means “anyway; anyhow”, indicating that for some reason the speaker cannot or is unwilling to tell the concrete situation but only tell the general fact or conclusion.

例如：上午有人给你打过电话，总之有人找过你。

5. 好，说走就走！

“说……就……”，“说”和“就”后面用同一个动词，这一结构表示动作快，毫不犹豫。

The construction “说……就……”, in which the same verb is placed after “说” and “就”, indicates that the somebody do something quickly and without hesitation.

例如：他很喜欢这件衣服，说买就买了。

6. 怎么像是站在了丁字路口呢？

“丁字路口”，指两条路纵横相接，像汉字“丁”的形状的路口。

“丁字路口” refers to the crossing of two roads connecting together to form the shape of the Chinese character “丁”.

例如：我家就在丁字路口附近。

7. 我可算是爬上来了。

“算”，副词，表示愿望终于实现了，有自我安慰的意思，后面常有“是”。

The adverb “算”, usually followed by “是”, indicates that one’s wish has come true at last and contains the meaning of self-consolation.

例如：这次考试，我算是过关了。

替换练习 Substitution Drills

1. 我来感受一下这里的	火热	气氛。		
	幸福	生活		
	春天	气息		
	欢乐	氛围		

2. 林则徐	真	是作出了	卓越	的贡献。
科学家	的确		伟大	
教师	确实		重要	
工人	毕竟		很多	

3. 新渠	修好	后，受益地区更广了。
新品种	推广	
税收	改制	
电站	建成	

会 话 Conversations

完成下列会话 Complete the following dialogues

（如括号里有词语或提示，请按要求做 Use the words or expressions given in the brackets）

A: 你看工地上真是热火朝天的。

B: ________________________。（起劲儿）

A: 修建这条水渠的经费是怎么来的？

B: ________________________。（捐资）

A: 我们也去参加义务劳动好吗？

B: ________________________。（说……就……）

A: 能到这里参加义务劳动还真不容易。

B: ________________________。（总之，白）

锡伯民俗风情园（一）

【第二十四集】

场景 Scene 锡伯民俗风情园民俗展厅

大　牛：请问主人在家吗？屋里有人吗？

韩　佳：大牛，你就别问了。这里啊，除了咱俩没有别人。

大　牛：哎，韩佳，你看。这张桌子上有饭菜，这家的主人肯定没走远。

韩　佳：嗯，有道理。

大　牛：那是啊！我大牛在推理这方面特别有天赋，就凭一点儿线索就能把事情猜个大概。

韩　佳：你可真是半道上捡个喇叭——有吹的啦[①]！

大　牛：什么叫吹啊？

韩　佳：那好吧。凭这饭菜，你倒是帮我推理一下，这是哪个民族的啊[②]？

大　牛：啊，就凭这点儿饭菜，猜主人的民族啊？

韩　佳：这肯定是锡伯族的朋友。

大　牛：锡伯族？你怎么看出来他们是锡伯族的呢？

Nǐ zěnme kàn chulai tāmen shì Xībózú de ne?
你 怎么 看 出来 他们 是 锡伯族 的 呢？

How can you tell that they're of the Sibo ethnicity?

韩　佳：就凭这张饼啊。这可是东北地区的特色食品，土生土长的新疆人啊是不做的。

大　牛：什么东北西北的？跟锡伯族没什么关系[③]。证据不足啊，证据不足。

韩　佳：哎，别动。

大　牛：怎么了啊？

韩　佳：你坐的这个地方啊就是第二个证据。你想想啊，在伊犁其他民族的家里哪家会有火炕啊？

Daniel: Is the owner of this house at home? Anybody in?

Han Jia: Daniel, stop asking. Here, except us, there's no one else.

Daniel: Eh, Han Jia, look. there is food on the table here, the owner of this house must be around.

Han Jia: Sounds reasonable.

Daniel: Of course! I have an exceptional gift for reasoning. Based on just a bit of clue, I can figure out an overall picture.

Han Jia: You must have stumbled upon a trumpet on your way—you have something to blow.

Daniel: I am not boasting.

Han Jia: Okay. Based on the food here, please make an inference regarding the ethnicity of this house owner.

Daniel: Just based only on the food here, you want me to guess the house owner's ethnicity?

Han Jia: They must be of the Sibo ethnic group.

Daniel: The Sibo ethnic group? How can you tell that they're of the Sibo ethnicity?

Han Jia: Only based on this pancake. It is the typical food in Northeast China. Native Xinjiang people normally don't eat it.

Daniel: Whether it's Northeast or Northwest China, it has nothing to do with the Sibo people. Insufficient evidence. Your conclusion lacks evidence.

Han Jia: Hey, don't move.

Daniel: Why not?

Han Jia: The place where you are sitting is the second evidence. Can you imagine there is an adobe bed in the Ili region in any other ethnic homes?

大　牛：哎，还真没有。哎，东北倒是挺多。

韩　佳：对啊。这些啊都是确凿的证据，证明这家的主人啊就是锡伯族的。

大　牛：你说他们是什么样的证据？

韩　佳：确凿的证据啊。确凿呢，就是指十分真实可靠。我们可以说确凿的证据，确凿的事实。

大　牛：你说的证据是挺真实的，不过都跟东北有关。跟锡伯族有什么关系啊？

韩　佳：因为锡伯族啊就是从东北迁居到这里来的，不过那是清朝[4]的时候了。

大　牛：哎，韩佳，主人还没回来，你干吗动他们的东西啊？

韩　佳：咳，你以为这里真的是一户人家啊？这里啊，是锡伯民俗风情园。这些吃的呢是特意为我们准备的。

大　牛：早说嘛。饿死我了。

Zhèxiē chī de shì tèyì wèi wǒmen zhǔnbèi de.
这些 吃 的 是 特意 为 我们 准备 的。

This food was prepared especially for us.

韩　佳：大牛，你慢点儿！慢点儿！

大　牛：味道真不错。

Daniel: No, I can hardly find any. But such adobe beds are quite common in Northeast China.

Han Jia: Right. These are all "quezao" proofs proving that the owner of this house is Sibo.

Daniel: What's the word you used before "proofs"?

Han Jia: "Quezao" proofs. "Quezao" means authentic and reliable. We may say "quezao" evidence, a "quezao" fact.

Daniel: The proofs you provided are authentic indeed. But they are both related to Northeast China. They have nothing to do with the Sibo people.

Han Jia: But all these Sibo people came from Northeast China during the Qing Dynasty.

Daniel: Eh, Han Jia, The owner hasn't come back yet, why are you touching their food?

Han Jia: Hey, you presume there is a real Sibo family living here? It is in fact part of the Sibo folklore garden. This food was prepared especially for us.

Daniel: You should have said that earlier. I'm starving!

Han Jia: Daniel, take it easy. Eat slowly.

Daniel: It's delicious.

场景 Scene 锡伯民俗风情园内

大　牛：哎，韩佳，刚才你还没说完呢。锡伯族怎么会从东北迁到新疆呢？

韩　佳：哦，当时的清政府啊从盛京，也就是今天的沈阳等15个城，抽调了锡伯族的官兵还有家属啊一共4000多人，来到新疆伊犁开垦荒地、守防边疆。后来啊，他们就留在这片土地上生活了。到今天为止啊，新疆的锡伯族人反而要比留在东北的锡伯族人还要多⑤。

大　牛：这下我明白了，难怪他们保留了那么多东北的传统⑥。

Daniel: Eh, Han Jia, you haven't finished your story yet. How come these Sibo people migrated from Northeast China to Xinjiang?

Han Jia: Well, the Qing government transferred 4,000 Sibo officers and soldiers and their families from Shengjing, or today's Shenyang, and 14 other cities to Xinjiang's Ili area to reclaim wasteland and defend the border region. And what happened later? They settled and started a new life here. And today, the number of Sibo people in Xinjiang is even larger than that of those remaining in Northeast China.

Daniel: Now I understand why they have retained so many Northeast customs.

场景 Scene 锡伯民俗风情园内

大　牛：韩佳，韩佳，我找到了一样好东西。

韩　佳：哦，什么东西啊？

大　牛：报纸。

韩　佳：报纸有什么稀奇的啊？不足为奇。

大　牛：韩佳，今天你在这儿用这个成语就不恰当了。

Jīntiān nǐ zài zhèr yòng zhège chéngyǔ jiù
今天 你 在 这儿 用 这个 成语 就
bú qiàdàng le.
不 恰当 了。

It is not appropriate for you to use that idiom here today.

大　牛：你看，这可是中国唯一的锡伯文报纸啊！就是一个字都不认识。

韩　佳：咳！

大　牛：这么难的语言谁学得会啊？

韩　佳：哎，你可别这么说啊。有人啊不光懂满、汉、蒙、锡伯等语言，而且呢还能用书法的形式表现出来呢[7]。

大　牛：还有这样的能人呢？

Daniel: Han Jia, I've found something nice.

Han Jia: Huh, what is it?

Daniel: A newspaper.

Han Jia: A newspaper is nothing strange or surprising.

Daniel: Han Jia, it is not appropriate for you to use that idiom here today.

Daniel: Look, this is China's only Sibo language newspaper. Pity I don't understand a single word.

Han Jia: Hey!

Daniel: It must be a complicated language. No one could learn it.

Han Jia: Eh, don't say so. There is someone who not only understands the Manchu, Mandarin, Mongolian and Sibo languages, but also is able to write in these languages calligraphically.

Daniel: Is there such a talented person?

场景 Scene 书画室

韩　佳：大牛，这位啊就是锡伯族著名的书法家格土肯先生。

大　牛：格先生，您好！

嘉　宾：你好！

大　牛：格先生，看您的意思，是不是想写我们的《快乐中国》？

嘉　宾：哎，不错。

韩　佳：《快乐中国》。今天啊，格老师给我们写了好多字。谢谢您啊。

大　牛：谢谢。哎，韩佳，别忘了这里还有一幅呢！

韩　佳：哦，对对对。啊？这是格先生写的吗？

大　牛：看不出来我还有这方面的潜力吧[8]？这锡伯文我也会写。

韩　佳：那这上面写的是什么啊？

大　牛：写的是“赏心悦目”。

韩　佳：咳，“赏心悦目”在这儿呢。

大　牛：啊？哦，请欣赏，请欣赏。

Han Jia: Daniel, this is the famous Sibo calligrapher Mr. Ge Tuken.

Daniel: Hello, Mr. Ge!

Mr.Ge: Hello!

Daniel: Mr. Ge, I guess you want to write "Happy China".

Mr.Ge: Yes, exactly.

Han Jia: "Happy China". Today, Mr. Ge wrote quite a lot for us. Thank you very much.

Daniel: Thank you very much. Eh, Han Jia, don't forget there is another scroll.

Han Jia: Oh, yeah. What? Did Mr. Ge write this?

Daniel: You don't think I also have potential for this? I can also write in Sibo.

Han Jia: What did you write on it?

Daniel: I wrote "Enjoyable Scenery".

Han Jia: Hey, *Enjoyable Scenery* is here.

Daniel: Yeah, please enjoy.

生 词 Words and Expressions

1. 推理	(动)	tuīlǐ	to infer; reason
2. 天赋	(名)	tiānfù	natural gift; talent; endowment
3. 线索	(名)	xiànsuǒ	clue; thread
4. 土生土长		tǔ shēng tǔ zhǎng	locally born and bred; born and brought up in the locality
5. 火炕	(名)	huǒkàng	heated *kang*; heated brick bed
6. 迁居	(动)	qiānjū	to change one's dwelling place; move
7. 民俗	(名)	mínsú	folk custom
8. 抽调	(动)	chōudiào	to transfer
9. 守防	(动)	shǒufáng	to guard; defend
10. 潜力	(名)	qiánlì	latent capacity; potential; potentiality

注 释 Notes

1. 你可真是半道上捡个喇叭——有吹的啦!

"半道上捡个喇叭——有吹的啦"，这是一句歇后语。"吹"有双关意思，表面上看是指"吹喇叭"，真实的意思是"吹牛"。关于歇后语，参见第十七集注释 1。

"半道上捡个喇叭——有吹的啦" is an allegorical saying. "吹" has a double meaning: the literal meaning is "to blow the trumpet", and the real meaning is "to talk big". As to the allegorical saying, please see Note 1 of Episode 17.

2. 凭这饭菜，你倒是帮我推理一下，这是哪个民族的啊?

"倒（是）"，副词，这里表示催促。

The adverb "倒（是）" is used to urge somebody to do something.

例如：车快开了，你倒快点儿走啊!

3. 什么东北西北的? 跟锡伯族没什么关系。

"什么……的"，这种用法表示否定，不同意对方说的话。中间引用别人的话并加以引申。

The construction "什么……的" is used to express disapproval or disagreement.

In the construction, what has been said by others is quoted and extended.

例如：什么北京南京的，每个城市都有自己的特点。

4. 清朝

清朝是中国最后的一个封建王朝（公元1616—1911）。满族人爱新觉罗·努尔哈赤所建，初名后金，1636年改为清。1644年定都北京。

The Qing Dynasty (1616—1911), the last feudal dynasty in Chinese history, was founded by Nurhachi, a Manchu. Originally it was called Later Jin, and changed to Qing in 1636. In 1644, Beijing was chosen as the capital.

5. 新疆的锡伯族人反而要比留在东北的锡伯族人还要多。

"反而"是连词，表示跟前面说的意思相反或出乎意料和常情之外，起转折作用。

The conjunction "反而", meaning "on the contrary; instead", indicates transition.

例如：春天来了，天气反而更冷了。

6. 这下我明白了，难怪他们保留了那么多东北的传统。

"下"，量词，"回""次"的意思，用于口语。"这下"即这次。

The measure word "下", used in oral Chinese, means "time". And "这下" means "this time".

例如：这下我们可要好好儿看看雪雕了。

"难怪"，副词，表示了解事物的真相后不再感到奇怪。

The adverb "难怪" indicates that after finding out the truth, the speaker no longer feels strange.

例如：难怪夜里那么冷，昨天外面是零下10度。

7. 有人啊不光懂满、汉、蒙、锡伯等语言，而且呢还能用书法的形式表现出来呢。

"不光……而且……"，这是一个递进复句结构，后一分句比前一分句表示更进一层的意思。

"不光……而且……" is a progressive compound sentence pattern. The latter clause has a further meaning than the former one.

例如：他不光会英语，而且法语也很好。

8. 看不出来我还有这方面的潜力吧？

“出来”是“看”的趋向补语，表示人或事物随动作由隐蔽到显露。肯定形式前面加“得”，也可以不加“得”，加“得”后句尾不能带“了”。否定形式加“不”。

As the complement of direction of “看”，“出来” indicates the process from concealment to revealment of a person or a thing with an action. The positive form can be preceded by “得”. If it is preceded by “得”，“了” can not be used at the end of the sentence. The negative form is “不出来”.

例如：这个人我认（不）出来了。

这个谜语我猜（不）出来了。

替换练习 Substitution Drills

1. 你怎么看出来	他们	是	锡伯族	的呢？
	我们		北京来	
	这些人		壮族	
	那些游客		广东	

2. 这些	吃的	是特意为	我们	准备的。
	水果		你们	
	衣物		灾民	
	书籍		战士	

3. 今天你在	这儿	用	这	个	成语	就不恰当了。
	会上	说		种	话	
	台上	唱		首	歌曲	
	课堂	讲		篇	文章	

会 话 Conversations

完成下列会话 Complete the following dialogues
（如括号里有词语或提示，请按要求做 Use the words or expressions given in the brackets）

A: 你们是泰国的游客吧？
B: ______________________________。（什么）
A: 对不起，你们是广西来的，我还以为你们是泰国人呢。
B: ______________________________？（看出来）

A: 新疆的锡伯族有多少人口？
B: ______________________________。（到……为止）
A: 锡伯族只讲锡伯语吗？
B: ______________________________。（不光……而且……）

锡伯民俗

锡伯民俗风情园（二）

【第二十五集】

场景 Scene 锡伯民俗风情园外

大　牛：哎，不好意思。快乐学汉语，轻松又好记。面对摄像机，哎，韩佳没了踪迹。哦，我知道她在哪儿。

场景 Scene 锡伯民俗风情园民俗展厅

大　牛：韩佳，我就知道你在这儿。不工作跑这儿来吃锡伯大饼，是不是？

韩　佳：当然不是了。我是来向导游小璞啊请教一些锡伯族民俗的问题。

嘉　宾：韩佳，你这么辛苦啊。这么早就来工作！

韩　佳：咳，干我们这一行的啊，早出晚归都已经成家常便饭了。习惯了。

大　牛：听听！听听！自己都承认是过来吃饭的。

韩　佳：什么啊？我说的是家常便饭。家常便饭啊，除了指家里的普通饭菜之外呢，还可以用来比喻十分平常、不足为奇的事情。

大　牛：“家常便饭”*字面意思指家里的普通饭菜，比喻十分平常、不足为奇的事情*。家常便饭。*例如*，对她来说，早出晚归就是家常便饭。我也一样。

Duì tā lái shuō, zǎo chū wǎn guī jiù shì jiācháng biànfàn.
对她来说，早出晚归就是家常便饭。

For her, going out early and coming back late is all in a day's work.

Daniel: Oh, I am sorry. Learn Chinese in the fun way. It's much easier to remember. With the camera here, but Han Jia is nowhere to find. Oh, I know where she is.

Daniel: Han Jia, I knew you must have been here. You put aside your work and came here to eat Sibo pancakes?

Han Jia: Of course not. I came here to consult tour guide Xiao Pu about some Sibo customs.

Guest: Han Jia, you are working so hard. You've already started to work so early!

Han Jia: Oh, for people in this profession, leaving home early and returning late is just "jiachang bianfan". I've been used to it.

Daniel: Hear! Hear! She herself has admitted coming here to eat.

Han Jia: What are you talking about? What I said was "jiachang bianfan". "Jiachang bianfan" means "a homely meal or simple food as well as something usual or nothing special".

Daniel: "Jiachang bianfan", literally home-made food, means "the old routine or nothing special". For example, for her, going out early and coming back late is all in a day's work. Me too.

新疆

韩　佳：是这样的。昨天啊，我发现了一样很有意思的东西。你看，就是这个。所以我今天啊特地来向小璞请教一下。

大　牛：是够稀奇的。这是干什么用的啊？

韩　佳：我想问，还没来得及问呢[1]。

大　牛：我还以为你都知道呢。

嘉　宾：还是我来给你们介绍一下吧。这个是锡伯族家中的家谱。

合：家谱？

韩　佳：哎，这家谱不是应该厚厚的一本吗？

大　牛：对啊，怎么可能是一条五颜六色的绳子呢？

嘉　宾：这真的是家谱。它叫喜利妈妈。你们看，每两块羊骨头之间就代表一代人。每一条布条就代表出生了一个女孩儿，而每一个小弓箭则代表出生了一个男孩儿，希望男孩子勇敢坚强，可以成为神箭手。

大　牛：有意思。

韩　佳：难怪锡伯族的人啊个个都善于拉弓射箭的。原来一出生就开始加以引导了。

嘉　宾：不错。我们这儿有许多可以射箭的地方。待会儿可以去试一试。

大　牛：好啊，好啊！射箭我拿手啊[2]！可是到哪儿去找箭呢？

韩　佳：哎，跟我来！

Han Jia: That's true. Yesterday, I found something very interesting. Look, it's this. So, today I came here especially to consult Xiao Pu.

Daniel: It does look rare. What is it used for?

Han Jia: I'm also wondering about it.

Daniel: I thought you already knew all about it.

Guest: Let me tell you. This is a Sibo genealogy.

Together: A genealogy?

Han Jia: Really? Shouldn't a genealogy be a thick book?

Daniel: Right, why is it just a colorful rope?

Guest: This is really a genealogy. It is called Mother Xili. Every two lamb bones represent a generation. And every strip of cloth represents a newborn girl while every bow and arrow represents a newborn boy, hoping boys will be brave and courageous enough to become good shooters.

Daniel: Interesting.

Han Jia: No wonder every Sibo man is good at archery. Actually they receive instruction soon after birth.

Guest: Exactly. There are many places for practicing archery here. You can have a try later.

Daniel: Terrific! Archery is my favorite sport. But where can I find a bow and an arrow?

Han Jia: Oh, come with me.

场景 Scene 做弓箭人家

大　牛：这么多弓箭！

韩　佳：是啊，这些可都是精弓利箭啊！您看，这位伊师傅啊就是一位做箭的高手。

大　牛：伊师傅，您好！

韩　佳：伊师傅，您好！

嘉　宾：您好！

韩　佳：大牛，你知道吗？在这里啊凡是勇敢的年轻人都有自己的弓箭[③]。

> Zhèli fánshì yǒnggǎn de niánqīngrén dōu yǒu
> 这里 凡是 勇敢 的 年轻人 都 有
> zìjǐ de gōngjiàn.
> 自己 的 弓箭。
>
> **All brave youngsters here have their own bow and arrows.**

韩　佳：你要不要也入乡随俗做一副啊？

大　牛：这个……其实啊我更想学一学古人。

韩　佳：学古人？好啊。哪位名将？

大　牛：不是名将，是名相——诸葛亮[④]。我要学他的草船借箭[⑤]。不用自己动手，就有弓箭送上门。

韩　佳：咳，你想得倒美！人家借箭靠的是智慧。你靠什么啊？

大　牛：我靠礼貌。伊师傅，打扰一下您的工作。可不可以向您借一副弓箭呢？

嘉　宾：可以，可以。就这把弓箭，这叫霸王弓。

韩　佳：霸王弓。

大　牛：嗯，不错。

Daniel: There are so many bows and arrows here.

Han Jia: Yeah, these are all nice bows and sharp arrows. Look, Mr. Yi is a top-notch arrow maker.

Daniel: Hi, Mr. Yi.

Han Jia: Hello, Mr. Yi.

Guest: Hi.

Han Jia: Daniel, do you know all brave youngsters here have their own bow and arrows?

Han Jia: Do you also want to make a set of your own as the saying goes: "When in Rome do, as the Romans do"?

Daniel: About this, I would rather learn from the ancient people.

Han Jia: Learn from the ancient people? Good. Which famous general?

Daniel: Not a famous general, but a famous prime minister, Zhuge Liang. I want to learn his strategy of borrowing arrows with straw boats. I don't have to use my own hands and I'll have them delivered to my doorstep.

Han Jia: Hey, you are daydreaming! Zhuge "borrowed" arrows with his intelligence. What do you have?

Daniel: I have my politeness. Mr. Yi, sorry to bother you, can I borrow a bow and an arrow from you?

Guest: Sure. This set of bow and arrow is called *Bawang* Crossbow.

Han Jia: *Bawang* Crossbow.

Daniel: Um, not bad.

场景 Scene 锡伯民俗风情园射箭场

大　牛：甭管怎么借来的，现在我总算有了精弓利箭[6]。可以好好跟锡伯族的朋友们比一比。

韩　佳：就你那箭术啊，锡伯族的姑娘们都比你强。

大　牛：太小瞧人了吧？

韩　佳：哎，你还别不服。瞧瞧！

大　牛：啊？

韩　佳：大牛，锡伯族是一个擅长射箭的民族，出了很多优秀的射箭运动员呢。

大　牛：嗯，她们的箭术的确不错，只可惜靶子不太结实，一旦被射中就散了[7]。

韩　佳：这你就不懂了吧，这是传统的靶子。箭射中哪一环呢，哪一环就会掉下来。

Jiàn shèzhòng nǎ yì huán, nǎ yì huán jiù huì
箭　射中　哪　一　环，哪　一　环　就　会

diào xialai.
掉　下来。

Any ring which is hit by an arrow will fall.

大　牛：原来是这样。我也来试试。一箭射出，哈哈，“赏心悦目”。

Daniel: No matter how I borrowed them, I have a strong bow and a sharp arrow. Now I can compete with our Sibo friends.

Han Jia: At shooting arrows, even Sibo girls are better than you.

Daniel: You are belittling me.

Han Jia: You refuse to give in? Try it.

Daniel: No!

Han Jia: Daniel, Sibo people are especially good at archery and many excellent archery athletes are of Sibo ethnicity.

Daniel: Their archery is really good. But it's a pity the target isn't firm enough. It collapses every time it is hit.

Han Jia: You don't understand this is a traditional target. Any ring which is hit by an arrow will fall.

Daniel: Oh, I see. Let me also have a try. I have shot out an arrow, ha-ha. The *Enjoyable Scenery*.

生 词 Words and Expressions

1. 踪迹	（名）	zōngjì	trace; track
2. 稀奇	（形）	xīqí	rare; strange; curious
3. 家谱	（名）	jiāpǔ	genealogy; family tree
4. 五颜六色		wǔ yán liù sè	of various colors; multicolored; colorful
5. 弓箭	（名）	gōngjiàn	bow and arrow
6. 善于	（动）	shànyú	to be good at; be adept in
7. 引导	（动）	yǐndǎo	to guide; lead
8. 高手	（名）	gāoshǒu	past master; master-hand; ace
9. 智慧	（名）	zhìhuì	wisdom; intelligence
10. 靶子	（名）	bǎzi	target

注 释 Notes

1. 我想问，还没来得及问呢。

“来得及”，表示还有时间，能够顾到或赶上。前面常用“还、都、也”。否定形式是“来不及”。

“来得及”, usually preceded by “还”, “都” or “也”, means “there's still time; to be able to do something in time; be able to make it”. And its negative form is “来不及”.

例如：火车 10 点开，时间还来得及。

2. 射箭我拿手啊！

“拿手”，意思是对某种技艺很擅长。

“拿手” means “adept; expert; good at”.

例如：做红烧肉他最拿手。

3. 凡是勇敢的年轻人都有自己的弓箭。

“凡是”，副词，总括在某一范围内的一切。后面一般有“都”与之搭配。

The adverb “凡是”, meaning “every; all”, always collocates with “都” in the latter part of the sentence.

例如：凡是新来的教师都要进行培训。

4. 诸葛亮

诸葛亮（181—234），三国时的政治家、军事家，曾担任刘备蜀汉的丞相。

Zhuge Liang (181—234) was a statesman and strategist in the Three Kingdoms Period and once held the position of the Prime Minister of the Kingdom of Shu Han in the reign of Liu Bei.

5. 草船借箭

这个故事见于古典小说《三国演义》。故事内容是：刘备和吴国的孙权联合抵抗江北曹操的进攻，情况紧急，需要十万支箭。诸葛亮准备二十只船，船用黑布遮盖，每只船上只用少数士兵，另外放上一千个草把子排在船的两边。趁大雾天气，诸葛亮将二十只船靠近曹操的阵地，并擂鼓喊叫。曹操因江上大雾，害怕有诈，不敢出兵，只叫士兵发箭射击。等大雾散去，草把子上插满了箭。

Borrowing Arrows with Straw Boats is a story from the classical novel *Romance of the Three Kingdoms*. The story goes as follows: Liu Bei and Sun Quan of the Kingdom of Wu united together to resist the attack of Cao Cao in the north of the Yangtze River. The situation was critical and they needed 100,000 arrows. Zhuge Liang prepared 20 boats, which were covered with black cloth. He ordered only a few soldiers to stay in each of the boats and 1,000 grass bundles to be placed on both sides of each boat. Taking advantage of the heavy fog, Zhuge Liang ordered the 20 boats to approach Cao Cao's campsite and let his soldiers beat the drums and shout loudly. Considering the fog over the river, Cao Cao worried that this was a fraud and didn't dare to dispatch troops but only asked his soliders to shoot arrows. When the heavy fog dispersed, they found that the grass bundles were inserted with numerous arrows.

6. 现在我总算有了精弓利箭。

"总算"，副词，意思是毕竟、终归。

The adverb "总算" means "after all; at last".

例如：一直盼望你来，今天你总算来了。

7. 只可惜靶子不太结实，一旦被射中就散了。

"一旦……就……"，这是条件复句结构。"一旦"，副词，表示有了某种条件，"就"表示随之而发生的结果。

The construction "一旦……就……" is a conditional compound structure. The adverb "一旦" introduces some condition, and "就" is the result.

例如：战争一旦爆发，人类就要遭受一场灾难。

替换练习 Substitution Drills

1. 对她来说，	早出晚归	就是家常便饭。
	起早贪黑	
	周末加班	
	深夜工作	

2. 这里凡是	勇敢	的	年轻人	都有自己的	弓箭。
	勤劳		农民		小楼
	参保		居民		医生
	富裕		学生		汽车

3. 箭射中	哪	一	环，	哪	一	环	就	会	掉下来。
球传到		个	人		个	人		要	站出来
货送到		家	商店		家	商店		立刻	收下
战士分到		个	单位		个	单位		必须	接受

会 话 Conversations

完成下列会话 Complete the following dialogues

(**如括号里有词语或提示，请按要求做** Use the words or expressions given in the brackets)

A: 我们去参观民俗展览好吗？

B: ______________________________。(来不及)

A: 时间还来得及，赶快去吧。

B: ______________________________。(说……就……)

A: 你们学校学生都有助学金吗？

B: ______________________________。(凡是……都……)

A: 那考试要是不及格怎么办？

B: ______________________________。(一旦……就……)

喀纳斯湖（一）

【第二十六集】

场景 Scene 野外

大　牛：快乐学汉语，轻松又好记。这可是我们的口头禅。我们今天来的这个地方也有一句俗话，叫阿尔泰山七十二条沟，沟沟有黄金。我可要发财了！

韩　佳：哎，大牛，又做什么梦呢？

大　牛：做什么梦啊？淘金梦。

韩　佳：哦，你也知道阿尔泰山有金矿啊？

大　牛：当然了，我消息灵通啊！

韩　佳：不过这个消息没什么时效性，可有点儿落伍了。

大　牛：什么意思？

韩　佳：人们早就不到这里来淘金了。现在流行到这里来赏美景，做驴友。

大　牛：啊，驴友？跟驴交朋友？

韩　佳：说你落伍了吧，连驴友都不知道？驴友就是旅游的谐音，就是指那些喜欢背行囊、住帐篷，进行户外自助旅游的朋友。

大　牛：原来驴友是指backpacker。这种旅行方式我也喜欢啊。那咱们今天就做一回驴友，一起去寻访神秘的喀纳斯湖，怎么样？

Ràng wǒmen qù xúnfǎng shénmì de Kānàsī Hú ba.
让 我们 去 寻访 神秘 的 喀纳斯 湖 吧。

Let's take a trip to the mysterious Kanas Lake.

Daniel: Learn Chinese in the fun way. It's much easier to remember. That's our pet phrase. In the place where we are today, there is also an old saying: "there is gold in all the 72 gullies of the Altay Mountains." I'm going to make a fortune!

Han Jia: Hey, Daniel, are you daydreaming again?

Daniel: Daydreaming? I'm dreaming of digging gold.

Han Jia: Huh, do you also know there are gold mines in the Altay Mountains?

Daniel: Of course I do. I am well-informed.

Han Jia: But this information is not up-to-date. It's a bit outdated.

Daniel: What do you mean?

Han Jia: People no longer come in search of gold. They come to enjoy the scenery as a "luyou" (companion on the journey, literally "donkey friend").

Daniel: What is a "luyou"? Making friends with donkeys?

Han Jia: You are behind the times. You don't even know what "luyou" is? "luyou" is homophonic to "luyou" (traveling), referring to those backpackers who camp outdoors while go sightseeing.

Daniel: As it turned out, a "luyou" is a backpacker. I also enjoy traveling in this way. Then, how about being a "luyou" for a day and visiting the mysterious Kanas Lake?

场景 Scene 路途中

大　牛：哎，我终于明白，为什么大家把喜欢自助旅游的人称作"驴友"了。

韩　佳：哦，为什么？

大　牛：驴子吃得简单，我们吃得也随意啊。驴子善于驮东西啊，我们这大包小包的，也不轻松啊。不过我觉得叫驴友还不如叫牛友。

韩　佳：啊，怎么讲啊？

大　牛：你想啊，驴子的这些优点我们牛全都具备。再说，小小的驴子哪有我们牛吃苦耐劳啊。

韩　佳：嗯，这的确是牛的优点。能吃苦又经得起劳累，我们可以用一个词来形容，吃苦耐劳。

大　牛：没错儿。吃苦耐劳*就是能吃苦又经得起劳累*。吃苦耐劳。

韩　佳：既然牛那么吃苦耐劳，又乐于助人，我看改叫牛友也行[①]。

大　牛：啊，别，别。韩佳，还是叫驴友吧，叫驴友合适。

Daniel: Oh, now I understand why people call backpackers "luyou".

Han Jia: Why?

Daniel: It's because a donkey eats simple fodder. And we also eat plain food. The donkeys are good at carrying things. And we also have lots of bags to carry. But I prefer "niuyou" to "luyou".

Han Jia: What do you mean?

Daniel: Just consider the fact that oxen have all the merits that donkeys have. Besides, the little donkeys are not as "chi ku nai lao" as oxen.

Han Jia: Yes, that's the merit of oxen indeed. We use "chi ku nai lao" to describe the fine quality of working hard and tirelessly.

Daniel: Exactly. "Chi ku nai lao" means "hardworking and diligent".

Han Jia: Since oxen are so "chi ku nai lao" and helpful, I suggest "luyou" be changed to "niuyou".

Daniel: Oh, no, no. Han Jia, let it still be called "luyou". "Luyou" is more suitable than "niuyou".

场景 Scene 路途中

大　牛：听说喀纳斯有“中国的瑞士”之称，特别令人向往。

韩　佳：这里独特的地理条件和气候条件使得喀纳斯的地理类型十分丰富。

Kānàsī de dìlǐ lèixíng shífēn fēngfù.

喀纳斯 的 地理 类型 十分 丰富。

There are many kinds of geographical terrain in Kanas.

韩　佳：这里植物群落都是依山而生的，层次分明。由下而上包括了山地草原带、山地森林带、草甸带、冰川恒雪带等等不同的生态圈。

大　牛：天哪，这么多！简直就是大自然赐给人类的一幅天然的地理和生态学的实验模型！

韩　佳：嗯，说得好！

大　牛：这里的地理类型这么多，动植物的种类一定少不了。

韩　佳：是啊。这里光植物就将近有800种，动物也有上百种。

大　牛：韩佳，你看老鹰！

韩　佳：咳，你往下看。

Daniel: I heard Kanas is billed as China's Switzerland, a very attractive place.

Han Jia: The special geological and climatic conditions here have resulted in diverse geographical terrains.

Han Jia: Floras are different on different levels of the mountain with clear distinctions. From the bottom to the top, there are different biospheres, such as alpine prairies, alpine forests, meadows, glaciers and permanent snow.

Daniel: My god, so many! It's simply a nature-endowed geographical and ecological exeperimental model!

Han Jia: Yeah, well put!

Daniel: With so diverse geographical features, there must be a good variety of flora and fauna.

Han Jia: That's true. Of plants alone, there are nearly 800 species. And there are about 100 kinds of animals.

Daniel: Han Jia, look, an eagle!

Han Jia: Hey, look downward.

场景 Scene 喀纳斯河边

韩　佳：大牛，你看！这就是喀纳斯河了。水的颜色就跟玉一样[②]。水流还挺急。

大　牛：都到喀纳斯河河岸了，肯定离喀纳斯湖不远。

韩　佳：咳，这才走了多远啊。还早着呢！估计今天是到不了喽[③]。

大　牛：这不是白忙活了吗？

韩　佳：不白忙，不白忙。今天到不了，说不定明天就能到了。

大　牛：还说不定[④]？

韩　佳：路是有点儿远，不过我们只要逆着喀纳斯河走，一定走不丢。你看，那不就是路牌吗？

大　牛：嗯，方向倒是没错。这些路牌可以防止游人不走冤枉路。

韩　佳：哎，打住！你刚才用“不、防止”两个否定词，那就变成肯定的意思了。那你的意思是那路牌可以让游人走冤枉路，是吗？

大　牛：不是，不是。我是多说了一个否定词。应该说这些路牌可以防止游人走冤枉路。

Zhèxiē lùpái kěyǐ fángzhǐ yóurén zǒu yuānwanglù.
这些 路牌 可以 防止 游人 走 冤枉路。

These road signs make sure that tourists don't go the wrong way.

大　牛：哎呀，我对喀纳斯湖可是充满期待。虽然还没有到，但是沿途的风光也不错。

韩　佳：那倒是[⑤]。驴友，我们赶紧上路吧！

大　牛：等等，等等。驴友也需要劳逸结合嘛。不如先看看我们今天的“赏心悦目”[⑥]。

韩　佳：好！

Han Jia: Daniel, look. This is the Kanas River. The color of its water looks like jade. And the currents are so rapid.

Daniel: Since we have already reached the Kanas River, we must be not far from Kanas Lake.

Han Jia: What? We haven't walked long. Still a long way to go. I presume we won't reach it today.

Daniel: Isn't this a futile trip?

Han Jia: No, it's not. If we can't reach it today, maybe we'll reach it tomorrow.

Daniel: And you are still not sure?

Han Jia: It's indeed a bit far, but as long as we walk upstream along the Kanas River, we'll not lose our way. Look, isn't that a road sign?

Daniel: Yeah, we're in the right direction. Such road signs "fangzhi" (prevent) travelers "bu zou yuanwanglu" (no vain trip).

Han Jia: Hey, stop! You used two negatives, "fangzhi" and "bu", which would become positive in meaning. Did you mean these road signs help people go an unnecessary long way?

Daniel: No, no. I used an extra negative. I should have said these road signs make sure that tourists don't go the wrong way. Oh, I am full of expectations of Kanas Lake. Although we haven't reached it, it's not bad to enjoy the scenery on the way.

Han Jia: Sure. Backpackers, let's hit the road!

Daniel: Wait, wait. Backpackers also need to strike a proper balance between work and leisure. We'd better watch today's *Enjoyable Scenery* first.

Han Jia: Good.

生词 Words and Expressions

1. 口头禅	（名）	kǒutóuchán	pet phrase
2. 淘金	（动）	táo jīn	to wash for gold; pan
3. 落伍	（动）	luòwǔ	to lag behind
4. 谐音	（动）	xiéyīn	homophony
5. 行囊	（名）	xíngnáng	traveling bag
6. 群落	（名）	qúnluò	community
7. 生态圈	（名）	shēngtàiquān	ecosphere
8. 赐	（动）	cì	to bestow; confer
9. 冤枉	（动、形）	yuānwang	to treat unjustly; wrong
10. 劳逸结合		láoyì jiéhé	to strike a proper balance between work and leisure; alternate work with rest and recreation

注释 Notes

1. 既然牛那么吃苦耐劳，又乐于助人，我看改叫牛友也行。

“既然”，连词，用在前一个分句，提出已成为事实的前提，后一分句常有“也、就、还”呼应，引出根据这个前提推出的结论。

“既然”is used in the first clause, introducing the prerequisite and the second clause, in which there is “也”, “就”, or “还” collocating with it. It is the conclusion drawn from the prerequisite.

例如：既然买了，也不必后悔，吃亏上当就这一次。

2. 水的颜色就跟玉一样。

“跟……一样”，这一结构用于比较两个人或两件事物性状的异同。基本句式如下：

The construction “跟……一样” is used to make a comparison between two persons or things. The basic pattern is as follows:

A	跟	B	一样。
这种瓜的味道	跟	蜂蜜	一样。

否定式有两种：

The negative form is "跟……不一样" or "不跟……一样".

这本书跟那本书不一样。

这本书不跟那本书一样。

3. 估计今天是到不了喽。

"了（liǎo）"在动词后跟"得、不"结合表示可能或不可能。"到不了"即不可能到。

"了（liǎo）", used after a verb plus "得" or "不", indicates possibility or impossibility. "到不了" means that it is impossible to arrive.

例如：我吃得／不了这么多菜。

4. 还说不定？

"说不定"，表示对情况没有把握，不能肯定。一般用在句子开头，也可以用在主语后。

"说不定", meaning "perhaps; maybe", is usually used at the beginning of a sentence and can also be used after the subject.

例如：说不定他不来了。

我说不定不去了。

5. 那倒是。

"倒"，副词，表示肯定，语气较舒缓。

The adverb "倒" indicates positiveness with a soft tone.

例如：这件衣服只花50元，那倒挺值。

6. 不如先看看我们今天的"赏心悦目"。

"不如"，动词，用于比较，表示前面提到的人或事比不上后面所说的。

The verb "不如", used for comparison, means "it would be better to".

例如：今天太热，别进城了，不如明天再去。

替换练习 Substitution Drills

1. 让我们去 寻访 神秘 的 喀纳斯湖 吧。

让我们去	寻访	神秘	的	喀纳斯湖	吧。
	游览	美丽		杭州西湖	
	看看	可爱		大熊猫	
	攀登	雄伟		长城	

2. 喀纳斯 的 地理 类型 十分丰富。

喀纳斯	的	地理	类型	十分丰富。
新疆		葡萄	品种	
中国		水果	种类	
西藏		矿产	资源	

3. 这些 路牌 可以防止 游人 走 冤枉路。

这些	路牌	可以防止	游人	走	冤枉路。
	说明		顾客	花	冤枉钱
	规定		客户	还	冤枉债
	法律		人们	吃	冤枉官司

会 话 Conversations

完成下列会话 Complete the following dialogues

（如括号里有词语或提示，请按要求做 Use the words or expressions given in the brackets）

A: 明天我们去游览喀纳斯河吧！

B: ______________________________。（……不了）

A: 没有汽车我们走着去。

B: ______________________________。（既然……就……）

A: 这里的风景实在太美了。

B: ______________________________。（简直，跟……一样）

A: 要能把家搬到这里来多好啊！

B: ______________________________。（说不定）

喀纳斯湖（二）
【第二十七集】

场景 Scene 喀纳斯河边

韩　佳：我和大牛跋山涉水终于来到了美丽的喀纳斯湖。瞧把他高兴的，高兴得连人影儿都没了①。

场景 Scene 观鱼亭

韩　佳：大牛，找什么呢？

大　牛：找鱼啊。这里不是著名的观鱼亭吗？可是这里这么高，就是有鱼也看不到啊②。

韩　佳：这你就有所不知了吧③？我们要看的可不是普通的鱼。

大　牛：那是什么？

韩　佳：是喀纳斯湖的湖怪。

大　牛：啊，这里有湖怪啊？

韩　佳：你别紧张，听我说完啊。有人说这湖怪是一种学名叫哲罗鲑的大红鱼。最大的有四米长、五百千克重呢。

大　牛：不会吧。喀纳斯能养出这么大的鱼？

韩　佳：至于这湖怪到底是不是这种鱼，现在还没有人敢确定④。不过我想这可能就是喀纳斯湖的神秘之处吧。

Zhè jiù shì Kānàsī Hú de shénmì zhī chù.
这 就 是 喀纳斯 湖 的 神秘 之 处。

That's what is so mysterious about Lake Kanas.

Han Jia: After crossing over mountains and wading through rivers, Daniel and I have finally arrived at the beautiful Kanas Lake. Daniel is so happy that he's disappeared soon after we got here.

Han Jia: Daniel, what are you looking for?

Daniel: I'm looking for fish. This is the famous Fish Observing Pavilion. But it's so tall, it will be difficult to see any fish from here.

Han Jia: This shows your ignorance. The fish we want to see is not an ordinary one.

Daniel: What's that?

Han Jia: It's a monster in Kanas Lake.

Daniel: What, a lake monster here?

Han Jia: Don't panic, let me finish. Someone said the lake monster is a kind of giant red fish, called Hucho taimen. The biggest is about four meters long, weighing 500 kilos.

Daniel: It's hard to believe. Could there be such huge fish in the lake?

Han Jia: Whether the monster is this kind of fish has not been confirmed by anyone. But I believe that's what is so mysterious about Kanas Lake.

场景 Scene 山路上

韩 佳：喀纳斯在蒙语里就是美丽富饶、神秘莫测的意思。怎么样，是不是又增添了几分神秘感呢？

大 牛：“神秘莫测”*的意思是非常神秘，谁也难以摸清底细。*神秘莫测。

韩 佳：没错儿。神秘莫测就是指非常神秘，谁也难以摸清底细。

大 牛：解释了半天，这个词语大家懂了。可是湖怪呢，在哪儿啊？

韩 佳：湖怪？这个……湖怪可能是等不着了⑤。我觉得咱们还是应该抓紧时间欣赏喀纳斯的美景。

大 牛：好。

韩 佳：走。

Han Jia: Kanas, in Mongolian, means "beautiful, rich and mysterious". Now do you feel some additional sense of mystery?

Daniel: "Shenmi mo ce" is a Chinese phrase which means "incredibly mysterious, fathomless".

Han Jia: Exactly. "Shenmi mo ce" means something is so mysterious that no one understands it.

Daniel: After your repeated explanations, we are all clear about it. But where is the lake monster?

Han Jia: The lake monster? Perhaps we may not have the chance to see it. I think we should take the chance to enjoy the scenery around Kanas Lake.

Daniel: Okay.

Han Jia: Let's go.

场景 Scene　喀纳斯湖边

韩　佳：我现在马上要为您揭晓喀纳斯湖最明显的一个神秘特征。

大　牛：什么啊？不会是见不着的水怪吧？你快讲讲吧。

韩　佳：不用讲。耳听为虚，眼见为实。你只要盯着那湖水看就清楚了。

大　牛：盯着湖水看哪？没什么特别啊。

韩　佳：它的特别之处就在于保证你每次来看这湖水，湖水的颜色都不一样。

Nǐ měi cì lái kàn húshuǐ, tā de yánsè dōu bù yíyàng.
你 每 次 来 看 湖水，它 的 颜色 都 不 一样。

Every time you look at the water here, you'll find it's a different color.

大　牛：湖水会变色，还真是够神奇的！韩佳，你也知道我大牛虚心好学。请教一下，为什么会这样呢？

韩　佳：这个嘛，有人说是由于水中矿物质的缘故，也有人说是因为光线的原因。

大　牛：咳，说了半天，你也没有为大家揭晓答案，还是个未解之谜。

韩　佳：哎，从另一个角度讲啊，这就更增加了喀纳斯湖的神秘魅力。

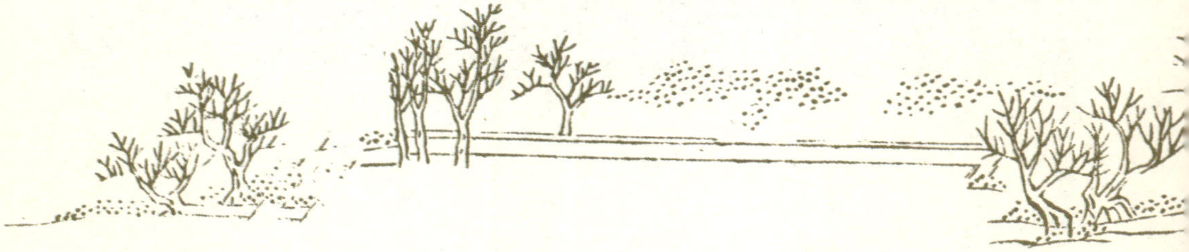

Han Jia: Now I'm going to tell you one of Kanas Lake's most salient mysterious features.

Daniel: What is it? Is it about the invisible lake monster? Tell us now.

Han Jia: You don't need me to tell you. Seeing is believing. Just stare at the water of the lake.

Daniel: I'm staring at the lake, but I don't see anything special.

Han Jia: What is special about it is that every time you look at the water here, you will find it's a different color.

Daniel: The color of the water can change. That's fantastic! Han Jia, you know I am modest and willing to learn. Please tell me why the color can change.

Han Jia: As for this question, some people say it is because of the minerals in the water. Others say it's because of the light.

Daniel: For all your explanation, you haven't given us the answer. It remains an unsolved riddle.

Han Jia: But if considered from a different angle, this just adds charm to this mysterious lake.

场景 Scene 游艇上

大　牛：这里的水怎么会变颜色呢？

韩　佳：你怎么还琢磨呢？紧接着又有一个神奇的景观出现在我们面前了。

大　牛：哦，什么呀？

韩　佳：你看，就是那边的枯木长堤。

大　牛：哪来的这么多木头？

韩　佳：弄不明白了吧？那我们就上去看看吧。

场景 Scene 枯木长堤

大　牛：不明白不要紧啊。我大牛可是全才啊！什么化学、建筑学我全懂。这条长堤是怎么修的、什么时候修的，我一会儿就能考证出来。

韩　佳：你真能看出来啊？确定吗？

大　牛：确定，当然确定了。

韩　佳：行了吧你，别打肿脸充胖子了⑥。这条长堤是自然形成的。

Zhè tiáo cháng dī shì zìrán xíngchéng de.
这 条 长 堤 是 自然 形成 的。

This long dam is a natural phenomenon.

Daniel: Why could the color of the water change?

Han Jia: You are still thinking about it? Now another magic spectacle is appearing before our eyes.

Daniel: What?

Han Jia: Look at that long dam of logs.

Daniel: Where did those logs come from?

Han Jia: You don't understand? Let's go up and have a look.

Daniel: It doesn't matter if I don't understand now. I am a versatile man, well-versed in chemistry and architecture. I am sure I can figure it out soon how this dam was built and when it was built.

Han Jia: Are you sure you can? Are you sure?

Daniel: Yes, I am sure.

Han Jia: Forget it. Don't pretend to be a know-all. This long dam is a natural phenomenon.

韩　佳：这里是喀纳斯湖的上游。这些枯木都是从下游被风逆流吹上来的。日积月累，积少成多，就形成了现在的这条枯木长堤。

大　牛：“积少成多”*就是说把点滴的东西积累起来也会变得很多。*积少成多。

韩　佳：嗯，没错儿。“积少成多”就是说把点滴的东西积累起来也会变得很多。就像我们学习汉语一样，每天学习一点儿，慢慢地您就会学得很好了。

大　牛：在这里我们祝电视机前所有的学汉语的朋友们——

合：好好学习，天天向上。

大　牛：可是韩佳，今天我们已经学得够多的了。能不能先放松一下？

韩　佳：你的意思是先看“赏心悦目”？

大　牛：没错儿。

Han Jia: This is the upper reaches of the lake. These logs were blown up here from the lower reaches of the lake. Many a little makes a mickle. Over time, a long dam of logs was thus formed.

Daniel: "Ji shao cheng duo" is a Chinese phrase, which means "to accumulate little by little".

Han Jia: Exactly. "Ji shao cheng duo" means "to accumulate". Just like learning Chinese, although we learn only a little each day, over time we'll learn the language well.

Daniel: Here we wish all our viewers learning Chinese from this program.

Together: Make steady progress every day.

Daniel: But Han Jia, we've already learned quite a lot today. How about a moment of relaxation?

Han Jia: You mean we watch the *Enjoyable Scenery* now?

Daniel: Exactly.

生 词 Words and Expressions

1. 跋山涉水		bá shān shè shuǐ	to scale mountains and ford streams—travel afar under difficult conditions
2. 底细	（名）	dǐxì	ins and outs; exact details
3. 揭晓	（动）	jiēxiǎo	to announce; make known; publish
4. 缘故	（名）	yuángù	reason; cause
5. 未解之谜		wèi jiě zhī mí	unsolved riddle
6. 魅力	（名）	mèilì	glamor; charm; enchantment; fascination
7. 琢磨	（动）	zuómo	to think over; turn over in one's mind; ponder
8. 考证	（动）	kǎozhèng	to make textual criticism; do textual research
9. 逆流	（动）	nìliú	to go against the current
10. 日积月累		rì jī yuè lěi	to accumulate over a long period

注 释 Notes

1. 瞧把他高兴的，高兴得连人影儿都没了。

“高兴”，形容词，后面加“的（得）”，放在句尾，后面的话说不出来，有无法形容的意思。句首都有“瞧、看”。

The adjective “高兴”, followed by “的” or “得”, is used at the end of a sentence and means “extremely glad” . At the beginning of the sentence, “瞧” or “看” is always used.

例如：这一次他考了一百分，瞧他美得！

2. 就是有鱼也看不到啊。

“就是”，连词，表示假设兼让步。后面常有“也”呼应，表示结果或说明。

The conjunction “就是” indicates assumption and concession concurrently. “也” is often used in the latter part of the same sentence to state the result or explanation.

例如：这点儿钱，就是他不还也没有关系。

3. 这你就有所不知了吧？

"有所不知"，意思是有的东西不知道（相反意思的词是"无所不知"）。"所＋动词"作为"有、无"的宾语。

"有所不知", opposite to "无所不知", means "there is something somebody doesn't know". "所 + verb" acts as the object of "有" or "无".

例如：你有所不知，他俩是亲兄弟，所以长得很像。

4. 至于这湖怪到底是不是这种鱼，现在还没有人敢确定。

"至于"，连词，表示另提一事。

The conjunction "至于", meaning "as for; as to", is used to mention something else.

例如：我们都愿意去黄山旅游，至于小张是不是愿意，我就不知道了。

5. 这个……湖怪可能是等不着了。

"着"，动词，用在动词后表示可达到目的。否定形式用"不"。

The verb "着" is used after a verb to indicate the attainment of the goal. "不" is used in the negative form.

例如：这种手机市场上能买着。
　　　这些资料我用不着。

6. 别打肿脸充胖子了。

"打肿脸充胖子"，这是一句俗语，字面上的意思是：本来不胖，把脸打肿了冒充胖子。用来比喻假装有本事、有能力，为了脸面硬要去做自己做不到的事。

The common saying "打肿脸充胖子" literally means that "to slap one's face until it's swollen to look imposing". It is a metephor which means "to puff oneself up to one's own cost".

例如：结婚没有那么多钱，就不要大操大办，别打肿脸充胖子。

7. 就像我们学习汉语一样，每天学习一点儿，慢慢地您就会学得很好了。

"像……一样"，"像"是动词，表示两个事物有较多的共同点，常和"一样、这样、那样"搭配。基本形式是：

像＋名＋一样＋形／动

In the construction "像……一样", the verb "像" indicates that two things share

a lot of things in common and often collocates with “一样”, “这样” or “那样”. The basic pattern is:

像 + noun + 一样 + adjective/verb

例如：上海的南京东路像北京的王府井一样繁华。

替换练习 Substitution Drills

1. 这就是	喀纳斯湖	的	神秘	之处。
	此人		可爱	
	佛教哲理		深奥	
	中国文化		博大精深	

2. 你每次来	看	湖水，	它的	颜色	都不一样。
	参观	展览		布置	
	买	水果		价钱	
	游览	北京		市容	

3. 这	条	长堤	是	自然	形成	的。
	场	灾难		海啸	引起	
	台	机器		中国	制造	
	块	疤痕		手术	留下	

会 话 Conversations

完成下列会话 Complete the following dialogues

（**如括号里有词语或提示，请按要求做** Use the words or expressions given in the brackets）

A: 听说喀纳斯湖非常神秘。

B: ______________________________。（连湖水……都……）

A: 湖里还有湖怪，说不定咱们能碰到呢。

B: ______________________________。（就是……也……）

A: 湖水的颜色怎么能变化呢？

B: ______________________________。（有所不知）

A: 你的解释难以让人相信，别再说了。

B: ______________________________。（那就，考证）

喀纳斯湖（三）
【第二十八集】

场景 Scene 白桦林

大　牛：韩佳，这么茂密的白桦林我还真是头一次看到。

韩　佳：嗯，我也是。感觉这一棵棵秀丽挺拔的白桦树就像一个个肃立的卫士一样。

大　牛：这个比喻好啊！好了，美丽的喀纳斯我们也看完了，现在应该收拾行装，背上大包回家了。

韩　佳：你以为看完了喀纳斯湖就完事了？这喀纳斯保护区散落着大大小小三百多个湖泊呢！

Kānàsī bǎohùqū yǒu sānbǎi duō ge húpō ne!
喀纳斯 保护区 有 三百 多 个 湖泊 呢！

The Kanas protection area has over 300 lakes.

大　牛：哦？比如……

韩　佳：比如有卧龙湾、月亮湾、神仙湾、鸭泽湖……

大　牛：好了，好了[1]。你就直说吧，我们先去看哪个？

韩　佳：看到这片白桦林，咱们就离卧龙湾不远了。

Daniel: Han Jia, this is the first time I have ever seen such a dense white birch forest.

Han Jia: Me too. I find these erect white birches look like soldiers standing guard.

Daniel: Nice comparison. Well, we've seen the beautiful Kanas Lake. It's time to pack up and go home.

Han Jia: You thought it's over after seeing the lake? There're more than 300 lakes, big and small, scattered around the Kanas protection area.

Daniel: Oh? Such as...

Han Jia: Such as Wolong Bay, Yueliang Bay, Shenxian Bay and Yaze Bay...

Daniel: Enough. You just say which one we are going to see first.

Han Jia: At the sight of the white birch forest, I know we are not far from Wolong Bay.

场景 Scene 卧龙湾

韩　佳：从大湖流出的喀纳斯河，曲折、奔腾了十公里之后，到这里又形成了一个湖。

大　牛：果然和喀纳斯湖一样美。

韩　佳：哎，你别光顾着欣赏，你倒是帮我找找，卧龙湾，卧龙湾，这龙在哪儿呢？

大　牛：龙啊？没找着，牛倒是有一头。

韩　佳：嘿，你又捣乱！

大　牛：开个玩笑嘛！我想他们说的一定是这块小岛。你看它细长的形状特别像一条龙。

韩　佳：大牛，你看那边。那就是号称“喀纳斯湖第一桥”的木桥。它可有上百年的历史了[2]。听说在那桥上可以看到卧龙湾最美的景色。

大　牛：百年历史的木桥啊？

韩　佳：你要是不去，我就跟观众朋友们去了[3]。

大　牛：哎，别别别。在我们《快乐中国》，我大牛最有团队精神了。我决定，我不仅要陪你一起去，而且我还要负责带路呢[4]！

Wǒ bùjǐn yào gēn nǐ yìqǐ qù, érqiě hái yào
我不仅要跟你一起去，而且还要

fùzé dài lù.
负责带路。

Not only am I going to accompany you, I'm going to lead the way.

Han Jia: Flowing from Kanas Lake, the Kanas River meanders and rushes forward for ten kilometers before forming another lake here.

Daniel: It does look as beautiful as Kanas Lake.

Han Jia: Hey, don't just enjoy the scenery. Please help me find out where the dragon lies in Wolong (Crouching Dragon) Bay.

Daniel: A dragon? No, I've found nothing except an ox.

Han Jia: Hey, you are getting mischievous again.

Daniel: I am kidding. I guess the place they said must be this isle. Look, its slender shape is like a dragon very much.

Han Jia: Daniel, look over there. That's the first wooden bridge in the Kanas Lake area. It's about 100 years old. It's said people standing on the bridge can see the most beautiful scenery of Wolong Bay.

Daniel: It's a 100-year-old bridge?

Han Jia: If you don't go, I'll go with our audience.

Daniel: Oh, yes, I'll go with you. Of all the *Happy China* staff members, I have the strongest sense of team spirit. I decide not only to accompany you, but also lead the way.

场景 Scene 木桥上

大　牛：真没想到，经过这么多年的风吹雨打，竟然还这么稳固啊[5]！

韩　佳：秘密就在于这座桥是用浸水后不腐烂、不变形的名贵红松做原料的。所以这座桥在水中耸立了上百年都完好无损。

大　牛：站在桥上从不同的角度看，景色也不一样。

韩　佳：是啊。这边呢是一平如镜的卧龙湾，而那边呢是奔腾咆哮的喀纳斯河。

大　牛：哎，韩佳，我记得这咆哮是说猛兽怒吼啊，你怎么说河水咆哮呢？

韩　佳：是这样的。“咆哮”可以用来形容河水奔腾、轰鸣。有时候呢也可以用来形容人暴怒、喊叫。

大　牛：“咆哮”，*“咆”读二声，“哮”读四声，用来形容河水奔腾、轰鸣；也可以用来形容人或野兽暴怒、喊叫。*咆哮。这下我彻底明白了。走，我们继续赏美景吧！

韩　佳：好吧。

Wǒmen　jìxù　xīnshǎng　měijǐng　ba!

我们　继续　欣赏　美景　吧！

Let's continue enjoying the scenery.

Daniel: It's amazing. Having been going through years of weathering, it remains so firm.

Han Jia: The secret lies in the fact that it's built with precious red pine wood, which does not rot or change in shape when submerged in water. Therefore, the bridge has remained in perfect condition despite 100 years in use.

Daniel: Standing on the bridge, I see different scenery in different directions.

Han Jia: Yes, indeed. It is the glassy Wolong Bay on this side and the "paoxiao" (roaring) Kanas River on the other.

Daniel: Eh, Han Jia, I remember "paoxiao" refers to the roaring of animals. But why did you say a "paoxiao" river?

Han Jia: Indeed. "Paoxiao" can be used to describe a boisterous river. Sometimes, it is also used to describe a person yelling in a rage.

Daniel: "Paoxiao", second tone, fourth tone, is an adjective which can be used to describe the roar of a rapid river, the roar of an angry beast or even the roar of an angry person. Now I am totally clear. Let's continue enjoying the scenery.

Han Jia: Okay.

场景 Scene 月亮湾

韩　佳：嫦娥奔月[6]。

大　牛：啊？嫦娥，在哪儿呢？

韩　佳：哎，往哪儿看呢？在那儿。

大　牛：啊，莫非它就是传说中的嫦娥[7]？

韩　佳：那是嫦娥的脚印。传说那两处浅滩就是嫦娥奔月留下来的脚印。

大　牛：我明白了，这里就是喀纳斯湖的标志景点之一——月亮湾了。

韩　佳：没错儿。

大　牛：月亮湾，月亮湾，它的形状还真挺像一轮新月。

韩　佳：新月是指月牙，不能用量词“轮”。一般来说圆形的太阳或者是圆月，我们才用量词“轮”。比如说一轮红日、一轮圆月。

大　牛：“轮”，*读二声，是一个量词，形容圆形的太阳或者是圆月。例如*，一轮圆月。那新月应该用什么量词呢？

韩　佳：用“弯”啊，一弯新月。

大　牛：哦，我知道了。一轮圆月，一弯新月。汉语的词汇真是太丰富了。

韩　佳：那当然。

大　牛：要说这嫦娥也真是的，这里有这么美丽的景色，她还往天上跑干吗呀？这里比月宫漂亮多了。

韩　佳：可不是嘛。看来大牛真是被这里的美景迷住了。那我们呢也帮他看看，看看这儿到底有多美。

Han Jia: Chang'e flying to the moon.

Daniel: Wow, Chang'e, Goddess of the Moon? Where is she?

Han Jia: Look in that direction. Over there.

Daniel: Is that the legendary Chang'e?

Han Jia: That's the footprint of Chang'e. It's said those two shoals are the footprints left by Chang'e.

Daniel: Now I understand this is one of Kanas Lake's scenic spots, Yueliang (Moon) Bay.

Han Jia: Exactly.

Daniel: The shape of Yueliang Bay is really like a "yi lun xinyue".

Han Jia: A "xinyue" refers to a crescent moon. So you can't use the measure word "lun" (something round) to modify "xinyue". We use "lun" only to describe the round-shaped sun or a full moon, for instance, "yi lun" crimson sun, "yi lun" full moon.

Daniel: "Lun", second tone, is a Chinese measure word for the full moon or the sun, for example, a full moon. Then what measure word should be used to modify a crescent moon?

Han Jia: We use "wan" (curved), "yi wan" crescent moon.

Daniel: Now I am clear. One full moon, one crescent moon. Chinese vocabulary is so rich.

Han Jia: Of course.

Daniel: Wasn't Chang'e a bit weird? With such beautiful scenery here, why did she fly to heaven? It is much more beautiful here than the moon.

Han Jia: Absolutely. Daniel seems enchanted by the scenery here. And we should also help him to find out how beautiful it is here.

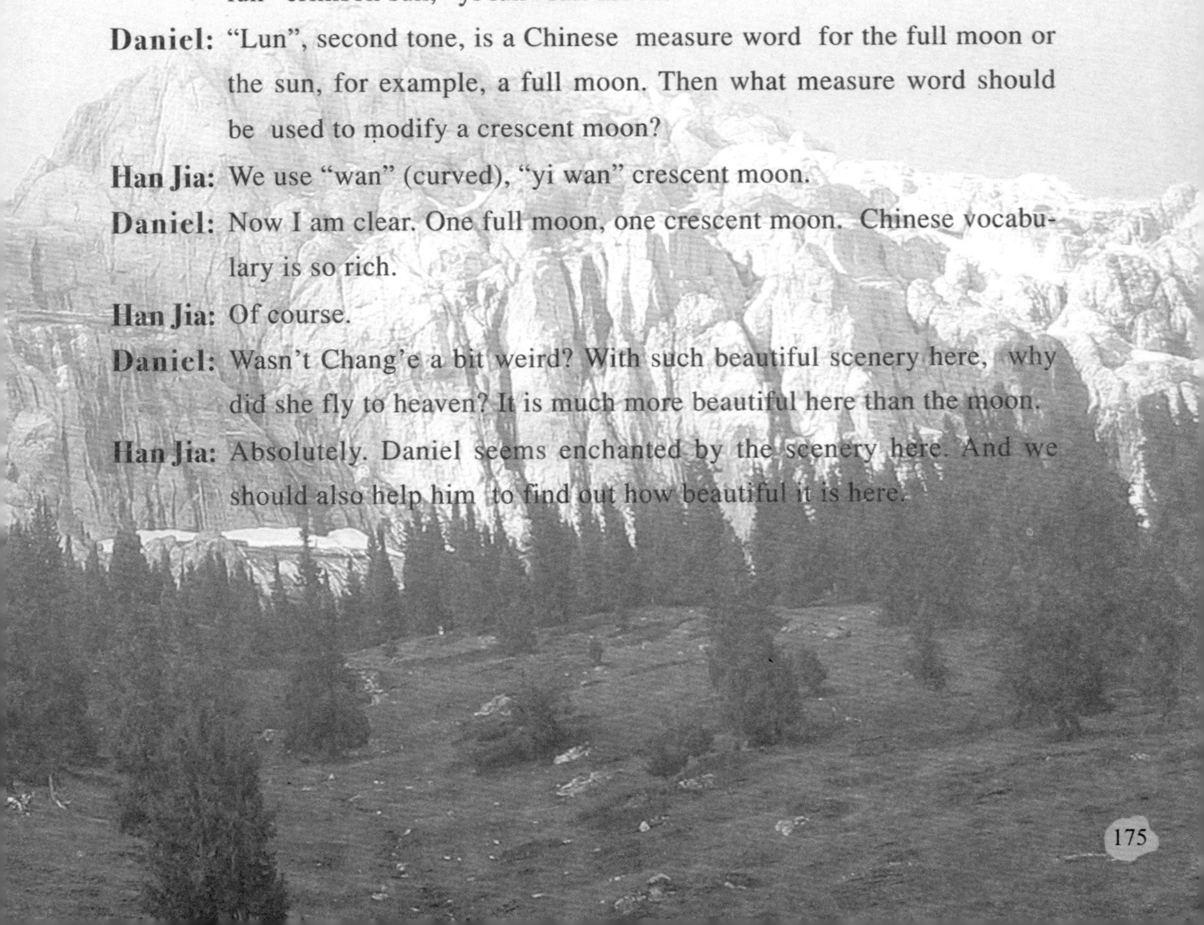

生 词 Words and Expressions

1.	秀丽	（形）	xiùlì	beautiful; pretty
2.	挺拔	（形）	tǐngbá	tall and straight
3.	肃立	（动）	sùlì	to stand as a mark of respect
4.	团队精神		tuánduì jīngshén	team spirit
5.	腐烂	（动）	fǔlàn	to decompose; rot
6.	耸立	（动）	sǒnglì	to tower aloft
7.	完好无损		wánhǎo wúsǔn	intact; whole; in good condition
8.	怒吼	（动）	nùhǒu	to roar; howl
9.	奔腾	（动）	bēnténg	to surge forward; roll on in waves
10.	浅滩	（名）	qiǎntān	shoal; shallows

注 释 Notes

1. 好了，好了。

“好了”表示制止继续说下去或做下去。连用两个“好了”语气更强。

“好了” is used to stop someone from talking or doing. And “好了，好了” expresses a stronger tone.

例如：好了，好了，就先做到这儿吧！

2. 它可有上百年的历史了。

“上”，动词，这里表示达到一定的数量，常带数量宾语。

The verb “ 上 ”, meaning “to be up to; as many as”, is often followed by a certain amount as its object.

例如：这个景点不错，每天都有上千人来参观。

3. 你要是不去，我就跟观众朋友们去了。

“要是……就……”，这是一个假设复句结构，“要是”提出一种假设，“就”引出在这种情况下出现的结果。

The conjunction “要是……就……” is used in an assumptive compound sentence, in which “要是” introduces a kind of assumption, and “就” introduces the result that the condition mentioned above may bring about.

例如：要是明天下雨，我就不去了。

4. 我不仅要陪你一起去，而且我还要负责带路呢！

连词“不仅”和“而且”呼应，构成的“不仅……而且……”结构，与“不但……而且……”的意义和用法相当，用于表示递进关系的复句中。“不仅”首先引出第一层意思，“而且”介绍出在程度上更进一步的第二层意思。

The construction “不仅……而且……”, whose meaning and usage are equivalent to those of “不但……而且……”, is used in a progressive compound sentence. “不仅” introduces the first clause, and “而且” introduces the second one, indicating a further meaning.

例如：这里不仅环境优美，而且交通也很方便。

5. 经过这么多年的风吹雨打，竟然还这么稳固啊！

“竟然”，副词，表示出乎意料，同“竟”。

The adverb “竟然”, equivalent to “竟”, means “out of one's expectations”.

例如：这么重要的活动，你竟然没去参加。

6. 嫦娥奔月

嫦娥是神话中的人物，为后羿的妻子。后羿从西王母那里得到不死之药，嫦娥偷吃后，便飞到月宫去了。

Chang'e, Goddess of the Moon, is a legendary character. According to the legend, she was Hou Yi's wife. After Hou Yi got the elixir from Queen Mother of the West, Chang'e had it secretely and then fled to the moon.

7. 莫非它就是传说中的嫦娥？

“莫非”，副词，这里表示怀疑、猜测。同“莫不是”。

The adverb “莫非”, equivalent to “莫不是”, indicates doubt or guess.

例如：莫非他生我的气了？

替换练习 Substitution Drills

1. 喀纳斯	保护区	有	三百多	个	湖泊	呢！
九寨沟	风景区		九		藏族村寨	
天津	开发区		几百		外资企业	
中关村	科技园		上千		公司	

2. 我不仅要跟你一起	去，	而且还要负责	带路。
	旅游		导游
	生活		照顾你
	上班		开车

3. 我们继续	欣赏	美景	吧！
	游览	长城	
	学习	英语	
	查阅	资料	

会 话 Conversations

完成下列会话 Complete the following dialogues

（如括号里有词语或提示，请按要求做 Use the words or expressions given in the brackets）

A: 你这次来新疆，印象如何？

B: ____________________。（不仅……而且……）

A: 要离开新疆，我真有些恋恋不舍！

B: ____________________？（莫非）

A: 哎呀，我还没有给朋友买些新疆的土特产呢！

B: ____________________。（竟然）

A: 光顾玩儿了，该办的事都忘了。

B: ____________________。（收拾）

喀纳斯湖（四）

【第二十九集】

场景 Scene 草地

大　牛：韩佳，等一会儿，我马上就好。

韩　佳：干吗呀？我要收帐篷啊，背上大包，继续我们的驴友之行——喀纳斯之旅。

韩　佳：大牛，真不好意思。我已经决定不当你的驴友了。

大　牛：那你一个人走行吗？

韩　佳：这你不用担心。我刚刚认识了几位摄友，就是爱好摄影的朋友。我决定跟他们一块儿走。真不好意思，先走了。

大　牛：哎，你怎么脱离组织啊？

场景 Scene 路途中

大　牛：您这个相机看上去挺高级啊[1]。

嘉　宾：这是专业的。

韩　佳：哎，大牛！

大　牛：韩佳！

韩　佳：你怎么……

大　牛：这么巧啊！你这是要去哪儿啊？

韩　佳：我们要去神仙湾拍照啊。那你呢？

大　牛：正好我也要去神仙湾呢。反正也是同路，干脆我们结伴而行吧[2]！

Gāncuì zánmen jié bàn ér xíng ba!

干脆　咱们　结　伴　而　行　吧！

Let's go together!

Daniel: Wait a minute, Han Jia. I'm ready in no time.

Han Jia: What are you doing? I am breaking camp and packing so as to continue our hike around Kanas.

Han Jia: Daniel, I'm sorry. I've decided not to be your travel companion this time.

Daniel: Are you sure you can travel alone?

Han Jia: Don't worry about it. I've just made friends with a few "sheyou", amateur photographers. I've decided to go with them. I'm sorry. I'm leaving now.

Daniel: Hey, how could you act independently of the team?

Daniel: Your camera looks pretty super.

Guest: It's professional.

Han Jia: Hey, Daniel!

Daniel: Hi, Han Jia!

Han Jia: How come?

Daniel: What a surprise! Where are you headed?

Han Jia: We're heading for Shenxian Bay for pictures. What about you?

Daniel: I am also going there. Since we are heading for the same destination, let's go together.

场景 Scene 喀纳斯湖

大　牛：哎呀，都说水是喀纳斯的灵魂。这话一点儿也不假。

韩　佳：没错儿。你看，在阳光的照射下，喀纳斯湖的湖水流光溢彩。那边的树叶还闪闪发光。

嘉　宾：哎，韩佳，这边景色好。快过来拍几张。

韩　佳：哎，来了。

大　牛：韩佳，等等，等等。你先帮我在这里拍一张吧，留个纪念。

韩　佳：这你就不懂了吧。我们搞摄影的人是专门拍景，不拍人的。

大　牛：那我自拍。

韩　佳：哎，你自己怎么拍啊？还是我来帮你吧。

大　牛：谢谢啊。

韩　佳：准备了啊。笑。哎，大牛，你在这儿慢慢玩儿。我们先走了。

大　牛：哎，你急什么呀？我知道鸭泽湖也叫野鸭湖。我对野鸭湖可是向往已久。

Wǒ duì Yěyā Hú kě shì xiàngwǎng yǐ jiǔ.
我 对 野鸭湖 可 是 向往 已久。

I've been looking forward to going to Wild Duck Lake for a long time.

韩　佳：大牛刚才说向往已久。向往就是说因为热爱或羡慕某种事物或境界，而希望得到或达到[③]。

Daniel: Wow, no wonder locals say water is the soul of Kanas. It's absolutely true.

Han Jia: Exactly. Under the sunshine, the water of Kanas Lake is resplendent with colors. And the trees over there also sparkle with light.

Guest: Eh, Han Jia, The scenery here is so good. Come over here and take a few shots.

Han Jia: Okay, I'm coming.

Daniel: Wait a minute, Han Jia. Please take a picture of me first as a memento of this trip.

Han Jia: Don't you know that as photographers, we only shoot scenery, never figures?

Daniel: Then I'll do it myself.

Han Jia: Hey, how can you do it yourself? Let me help you.

Daniel: Thanks.

Han Jia: Ready. Smile. Eh, Daniel, take your time and enjoy yourself here. The rest of us will go.

Daniel: Hey, what's the hurry? I know Yaze Lake is also called Wild Duck Lake. I've been looking forward to going there for a long time.

Han Jia: Daniel said just now "xiangwang yi jiu". By "xiangwang" he means that someone loves or admires something or someplace so much that he hopes to get it or reach it.

场景 Scene 野鸭湖

大　牛：韩佳，我看这里一定是野鸭湖吧。那里有野鸭子，我看得有十多只左右吧。

韩　佳：哎，你这句话可有问题啊。十多和左右都是表示大概的数字。十多只肯定是表示十只以上。十只左右既可以表示十只以下，也可以表示十只以上[4]。所以你用一个就够了。

大　牛：哦，我看得有十只左右。这回对了吧？

韩　佳：对。在这片湿地上，不光有成群结队的野鸭，运气好的话呢，还能看到很多种其他的鸟[5]。对了，我得去多拍几张。

大　牛：韩佳，你看那些野鸭子那么悠然自得！我们拍照别吓着它们。

韩　佳：咳，放心吧。我会离它们远远的，不会靠近的，我有这个。

大　牛：其实啊，我这个也有推拉的功能。

韩　佳：哦，哎，好好儿的，怎么不拍了呀？

Hǎohāor de,　nǐ　zěnme　bù　pāi　le?
好好儿 的，你 怎么 不 拍 了？

Everything's fine, why don't you take a photo?

大　牛：不是。我这个镜头怎么一推上去就不稳了呢？

嘉　宾：大牛，你这缺了个三角架。有三角架就稳了。你看我们怎么拍的。

大　牛：看来他们包里的东西也是必不可少的家伙啊。三角架啊，三角架。要不摄像师您受累，这个三角架借我用用好吧？想什么呢？

Daniel: Han Jia, I presume this must be Wild Duck Lake. There are wild ducks over there, at least about more than ten.

Han Jia: Hey, something wrong with your sentence. Both "shi duo" and "zuo you" mean an approximate number. "Shi duo" means definitely more than ten. "Shi zhi zuo you" may mean both less than ten and more than ten. So you should have used only one modifier.

Daniel: Oh, I presume "shi zhi zuo you" (about ten). Am I right this time?

Han Jia: Yes, you are. In this wetland, there are not only flocks of wild ducks, if you are lucky, you'll see many other kinds of birds. Oh, yeah, I'd better go take some pictures now.

Daniel: Han Jia, look how leisurely those wild ducks are! We mustn't scare them when taking pictures.

Han Jia: Yeah, rest assured. I'll keep quite a distance from them. I won't be too close to them because I have this camera.

Daniel: In fact, my camera also has zoom-in and zoom-out functions.

Han Jia: Huh, everything's fine,why don't you take a photo?

Daniel: Not that. My camera won't stay stable when in zoom-in mode.

Guest: Daniel, you need a tripod. It'll stay stable with a tripod. Look how we are taking pictures.

Daniel: I guess it's one of the indispensable gadgets in their bag. A tripod, yeah, a tripod. I have to bother you, cameraman. Would you please lend this tripod to me? What are you thinking about?

场景 Scene 草地

韩　佳：拍了不少照片，也看了不少美景。路也走了不少。我现在有点儿……

大　牛：饿了是吧？要想在野外吃东西，还是得靠我这个包里的东西⑥。

韩　佳：嗬！大家来，吃饭了啊！

嘉　宾：我们也带了。

大　牛：那正好，我们今天就来一个驴友、摄友大聚餐，怎么样？

韩　佳：好啊，好啊！不过在吃饭之前我们先来消遣一下，看看今天的"赏心悦目"。

Han Jia: I've taken a lot of pictures, seen a lot of scenery, and also walked a lot. Now I feel a bit ...

Daniel: Hungry? If you want a picnic here, you have to rely on things in my bag.

Han Jia: Wow! Come on, everybody. It's lunchtime.

Guests: We have food.

Daniel: Good, let's just have a big meal together with our "luyou" and "sheyou". What do you think?

Han Jia: Good, terrific! But before our meal, we'd better relax a while by watching today's *Enjoyable Scenery*.

生 词 Words and Expressions

1. 脱离	（动）	tuōlí	to separate oneself from
2. 结伴而行		jié bàn ér xíng	to go or travel in a group
3. 灵魂	（名）	línghún	soul
4. 流光溢彩		liú guāng yì cǎi	resplendent with colors
5. 向往已久		xiàngwǎng yǐ jiǔ	to look forward to for a long time
6. 羡慕	（动）	xiànmù	to admire; envy
7. 境界	（名）	jìngjiè	extent reached; state; realm
8. 成群结队		chéng qún jié duì	in crowds
9. 悠然自得		yōurán zìdé	to be carefree and content
10. 消遣	（动）	xiāoqiǎn	to divert oneself; relax

注 释 Notes

1. 您这个相机看上去挺高级啊。

“看上去”,“上去”是动词“看”的补语,“看上去”表示从外表估计、打量。

The construction “看上去”, in which “上去” is the complement of the verb “看”, means “estimating or judging from the appearance”.

例如：他长得真年轻，看上去不过二十来岁。

2. 反正也是同路，干脆我们结伴而行吧！

“反正”，副词，强调在任何情况下，结论或结果都不会改变。

The adverb “反正” emphasizes that no matter what happens, the conclusion or result will not change.

例如：要去你自己去，反正我不去。

3. 因为热爱或羡慕某种事物或境界，而希望得到或达到。

在“因为……而……”结构中，“因为”表示原因，“而”连接由此出现的情况或产生的结果。

In the construction “因为……而……”, “因为” indicates the cause, and “而” connects with the situation or the result arising therefrom.

例如：网球比赛因为大雨而中断了。

4. 十只左右既可以表示十只以下，也可以表示十只以上。

“既……也……”这一结构，连接两个结构相同或相似的词语，“也”引出的部分表示进一步补充说明。

The construction “既……也……” is used to connect two words or phrases similar in structure and what is introduced by “也” is used to further supplement and explain the subject.

例如：他既会英语，也会汉语。

5. 在这片湿地上，不光有成群结队的野鸭，运气好的话呢，还能看到很多种其他的鸟。

“不光”，连词，常跟“而且、并且、还”等搭配，组成递进复句，后面的成分表示意思更进一层。

The conjunction “不光” often collocates with “而且”, “并且”, “还”, etc. to form a progressive compound sentence of two or more clauses. The meaning of the latter part of the sentence goes a step further.

例如：我们学校不光有韩国学生，还有日本、泰国等国家的学生。

6. 要想在野外吃东西，还是得靠我这个包里的东西。

“要……还是得……”，在这个结构中，“要”表示假设，“还是得”强调实现“假设”必须的条件。

In the construction “要……还是得……”, “要” indicates assumption, and “还是得” emphasizes the necessary condition to realize the assumption.

例如：要取得成功，还是得靠勤奋努力。

替换练习 Substitution Drills

1. 干脆咱们 结伴而行 吧！
   不要去了
   大伙儿都去
   打道回府

2. 我对 野鸭湖 可是向往已久。
   九寨沟
   长城
   泰山

3. 好好儿的，你 怎么 不 拍 了？
   为什么 干
   因为什么 学
   干吗 参加

会 话 Conversations

完成下列会话 Complete the following dialogues
（如括号里有词语或提示，请按要求做 Use the words or expressions given in the brackets）

A: 你看大牛今天打扮得真年轻。
B: ______________________。（看上去）
A: 大牛，小韩今天怎么没来？
B: ______________________。（因为……而……）

A: 大牛，给我们拍个照好吗？
B: ______________________。（要……还是得……）
A: 给我们拍好啊！
B: ______________________。（既……也……）

图瓦风情
【第二十集】

场景 Scene 喀纳斯村村外

大　牛：您好，劳驾，喀纳斯村怎么走？我是说，喀纳斯村怎么走？

韩　佳：大牛，你们俩还在比画什么呢？

大　牛：哎，韩佳，你可算来了①。我找不到喀纳斯村，他说话我又听不懂。

韩　佳：听不懂你还看不懂啊？他的意思就是喀纳斯村在下面呢。

大　牛：啊，到了。

场景 Scene 喀纳斯村村内

大　牛：韩佳，刚才那位村民说的是什么语言啊？

韩　佳：他可不止说了一种语言呢。他用了图语和蒙语。

大　牛：这图语就是我们今天要拜访的图瓦族的语言。

韩　佳：没错儿。他们平时交流的时候用图语，学校的孩子上课用蒙文，和周边的哈萨克人交流时就会用哈语。

大　牛：每个人会三到四种语言呢！真厉害！真是能说会道。

韩　佳：你怎么张口就来啊②？“能说会道”不是指会很多种语言，而是指某人很善于言辞，很会说话。

大　牛：“能说会道”*指某人很善于言辞，很会说话*。能说会道。哎，这不是说我呢吗？开玩笑。今天我总算碰到比我有语言天赋的人了。

Wǒ zǒngsuàn pèngdào bǐ wǒ yǒu yǔyán tiānfù de rén le.
我 总算 碰到 比 我 有 语言 天赋 的 人 了。

Finally, I've found someone who is more talented with languages than I am.

Daniel: Excuse me, can you tell me how to get to Kanas Village? I mean in which direction I should go to Kanas Village.

Han Jia: What are you gesturing about with him?

Daniel: Oh, Han Jia, so good to see you here. I can't find the way to Kanas Village and I don't understand what he says.

Han Jia: But you should have understood his gesture even if you don't understand what he says. He means Kanas Village is down below.

Daniel: Oh, here we are.

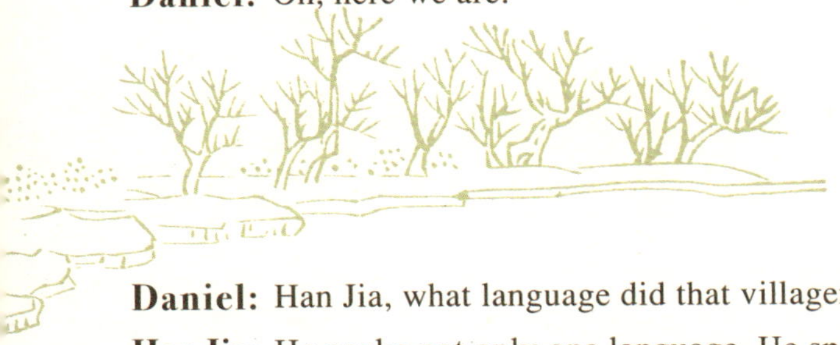

Daniel: Han Jia, what language did that villager speak?

Han Jia: He spoke not only one language. He spoke both Daur and Mongolian.

Daniel: Daur is the language spoken by the Daur ethnic minority, which we're going to visit today.

Han Jia: Exactly. Normally they communicate with themselves in Daur. Schoolchildren use Mongolian at school. When they communicate with their Kazak neighbors, they speak Kazak.

Daniel: Everyone can speak three to four languages! Fantastic! They are really "neng shuo hui dao".

Han Jia: You are so quick-tongued. But "neng shuo hui dao" does not mean "to understand several languages". It means "to be eloquent or glib-tongued".

Daniel: "Neng shuo hui dao" is a Chinese expression which means "to be a gifted orator or to have the gift of gabbling". Oh, does this refer to me? Just kidding. Finally, I've found someone who is more talented with languages than I am.

场景 Scene　喀纳斯村村内

大　牛：韩佳你看，敖包！那不是蒙古族的吗？

韩　佳：是啊。这图瓦人啊，据说是当年成吉思汗西征遗留下来的部分士兵逐渐繁衍起来的。

大　牛：哦，原来是这样[3]。

韩　佳：其实最有图瓦族特色的是那些散落在村中的小木屋。

大　牛：我才刚刚发现，松木的屋脊、松木的墙壁，连这围栏都是松木做的。真有特色！

韩　佳：哎，你听！更有特色的在那儿呢。

场景 Scene　喀纳斯湖边

大　牛：听上去很古老啊[4]！韩佳，这是什么乐器？

韩　佳：这就是图瓦人的传统乐器——楚乌尔，是用当地的一种植物做成的。

大　牛：我看看。真是太神奇了！只有三个孔，竟然还能吹出这么动听的乐曲。

韩　佳：所以说图瓦人也是音乐高手。

大　牛：韩佳，我想让这位先生教教我演奏楚乌尔。

韩　佳：那你可找对人了。这位先生在当地演奏是非常有名的。跟他学肯定学得快。

大　牛：这么多种乐器，我们慢慢学吧。

Daniel: Han Jia, an *aobao*! Isn't that dwelt by Mongolian people?

Han Jia: Yeah. It's said these Daurs here were descendants of Genghis Khan's westward expeditionary troops.

Daniel: Oh, I see.

Han Jia: In fact, the most salient Daur ethnic features are shown by those little wooden houses scattered in the village.

Daniel: I just found that the roof, the walls and even the fences are all built with pine timber. Very peculiar!

Han Jia: Hey, listen. The more peculiar thing is over there.

Daniel: Sounds very ancient! Han Jia, what kind of musical instrument is it?

Han Jia: This is the traditional musical instrument—the *chuwu'er*. It is made of a local plant.

Daniel: Let me have a look. It's fantastic! With only three holes, it can produce such a melodious tune.

Han Jia: So the Daurs are also talented musicians.

Daniel: Han Jia, I am wondering if this gentleman will teach me to play the *chuwu'er*.

Han Jia: You have found the right person. This gentleman is a well-known *chuwu'er* player. You'll make rapid progress if you learn from him.

Daniel: There are so many different kinds of instruments for us to study at our leisure.

Zhème duō zhǒng yuèqì, wǒmen mànmān xué ba!
这么 多 种 乐器，我们 慢慢 学 吧！

So many different kinds of instruments, we can study them at our leisure.

大　牛：韩佳，你觉得我吹得怎么样啊？
韩　佳：你啊还算说得过去。
大　牛：说得过去？去哪儿啊？
韩　佳：“说得过去”是指还可以，比较满意。
大　牛：“说得过去”*是指还可以，比较满意。*说得过去。
韩　佳：大牛，刚才都学了半天了，我有点儿口渴了。
大　牛：我好像闻到了一股香味。
韩　佳：香味？

Daniel: Han Jia, how do you think of my playing the instrument?

Han Jia: Just "shuo de guoqu" (passable).

Daniel: "Shuo de guoqu"? Where to?

Han Jia: "Shuo de guoqu" means "passable, relatively satisfactory".

Daniel: "Shuo de guoqu" is a Chinese expression, which means "average or satisfactory".

Han Jia: Daniel, we've been learning for quite a while, I feel a bit thirsty.

Daniel: I seem to have smelt a kind of aroma.

Han Jia: Aroma?

场景 Scene 图瓦人家

韩　佳：大牛，你的鼻子还真灵。这就是图瓦人制奶酒的容器。

Zhè shì Túwǎrén zhìzuò nǎijiǔ de róngqì.
这 是 图瓦人 制作 奶酒 的 容器。

This is a vat which the Daur people use to ferment milk wine.

大　牛：这么大怎么用啊？

韩　佳：其实啊，很简单。先把发酵的牛奶装到里面煮沸，让它变成蒸气。

大　牛：哦，*这个容器是做蒸馏用的。*用的是蒸馏的方法，对不对？

韩　佳：你还真说对了。其实这奶酒指的就是蒸气，它在这个封闭的容器里面变成水珠，然后就顺着这根特制的管子流出来。

大　牛：然后一碗新鲜的奶酒就做好了。

韩　佳：哎，大牛，要不然你也自己试试[5]？

大　牛：这么新鲜的奶酒当然要尝一尝了。

韩　佳：咳，我说的是让你试着做做。谁让你喝了呀？

大　牛：哎哟，不好意思，理解错了。我怎么补偿你呢？

韩　佳：哎呀，别补偿我了。你还是带着电视机前的观众朋友们，去了解一下图瓦人的民俗风情吧。

大　牛：没问题。您往那儿看。

Han Jia: Daniel, you have a sharp nose. This is a vat which the Daur people use to ferment milk wine.

Daniel: It's so big. How do they use it?

Han Jia: Actually, it's very simple. First pour the fermented milk into it. Then boil it on fire to distill it.

Daniel: I see. This vat is used for distillation. They use a distilling method, right?

Han Jia: You are right. Actually, the milk wine refers to a kind of vapor, which becomes tiny droplets in a sealed vessel. Then the liquid flows out through this tube.

Daniel: Thus a bowl of fresh milk wine is made.

Han Jia: Eh, Daniel, What about having a try yourself?

Daniel: I'll surely take a sip of such fresh milk wine.

Han Jia: Hey, I want you to try and make the wine yourself. I didn't ask you to drink it.

Daniel: Oh, I am sorry. A misunderstanding. What should I do for you as a compensation?

Han Jia: Hey, not for me. You'd better take our viewers on a trip to understand Daur people's customs.

Daniel: No problem. Look in that direction, please.

生 词 Words and Expressions

1. 比画（动）	bǐhua	to gesture; gesticulate
2. 言辞（名）	yáncí	words; utterance
3. 繁衍（动）	fányǎn	to multiply; increase gradually in number or quantity
4. 动听（形）	dòngtīng	melodious or pleasant to hear
5. 演奏（动）	yǎnzòu	to give an instrumental performance; play a musical instrument
6. 煮沸（动）	zhǔfèi	to boil
7. 容器（名）	róngqì	container; vessel
8. 蒸馏（动）	zhēngliú	to distill
9. 封闭（动）	fēngbì	to seal
10. 补偿（动）	bǔcháng	to compensate; make up

注 释 Notes

1. 你可算来了。

“算”，副词，表示期待很久的事终于实现了。前面加“可”语气更强。

The adverb “算” indicates that something one has been expecting for a long time has come true at last. And it can be preceded by “可” to express a stronger tone.

例如：这本书我可算买到了。

2. 你怎么张口就来啊？

“张口就来”是一种口语说法，指别人讲话太随便，不经慎重考虑。

The colloquial expression “张口就来” means “to talk carelessly and without prudent consideration”.

例如：他说话老是张口就来，不考虑影响。

3. 原来是这样。

“原来”，副词，表示发现了以前不知道的情况，含有恍然醒悟的意思。

The adverb“原来”indicates that the formerly-unknown situation has been discovered.

例如：我以为他出国留学去了，原来他还在北京。

4. 听上去很古老啊！

“上去”，这里是动词“听”的补语，表示对动作所涉及的事物作出判断。

“上去”is used as the complement of the verb“听”to indicate that judgement is to be made towards the thing the verb involves.

例如：这首歌听上去像新疆民歌。

5. 要不然你也自己试试？

“要不然”，连词，意思是“如果不这样”“否则”，引进表示结果或结论的句子。也可以说“不然”或“要不”。

The conjunction“要不然”, also“不然”or“要不”, meaning“if not”or“otherwise”, is used to introduce a sentence denoting a result or conclusion.

例如：你给他打个电话吧，要不然他会着急的。

替换练习 Substitution Drills

1. 我总算	碰到	比我有	语言天赋	的人了。
	找到		艺术才能	
	聘到		专业特长	
	请到		管理经验	

2. 这么多种	乐器，	我们慢慢	学	吧。
	衣服		挑	
	饺子		吃	
	报纸		看	

3. 这是	图瓦人	制作	奶酒	的	容器。
	藏族人		糌粑		工具
	西方人		布丁		原料
	中国人		年糕		木棰

会 话 Conversations

完成下列会话 Complete the following dialogues

（如括号里有词语或提示，请按要求做 Use the words or expressions given in the brackets）

A: 大牛，你来中国很久了，学会包饺子了吗？

B: ________________________________。（还）

A: 那现在我来教你怎么包。

B: ________________________________。（原来）

A: 你们西方的奶酪是怎么制作的？

B: ________________________________。（说实话）

A: 你真差劲儿，什么都不会！

B: ________________________________。（要不然）

新疆旅游指南

最宜人的季节

八九月份

不可错过的地方

果子沟、赛里木湖、天山天池、葡萄沟、火焰山、喀什香妃墓、楼兰城、喀纳斯湖、巴音布鲁克天鹅湖、唐布拉

最舒适的着装

运动装或休闲装

机场距市中心路程

乌鲁木齐地窝堡机场距市中心16.8公里

不可不尝的地方美食

大盘鸡、羊肉串、馕、手抓饭、拉条子

独一无二的特产

哈密瓜、葡萄干、无花果、天山雪莲

特别提示

1.新疆是中国最大的省份，地广人稀。与其他旅游地方不同，通常来新疆旅游是先到乌鲁木齐，再乘其他交通工具去各目的地。对于自助游的散客来讲，可以在当地租用汽车去各景点，也可以报名参加当地的旅行社组团。

2.新疆气候早晚温差大，出门时最好多带一些衣物；日照时间长，注意防紫外线；天气多变，注意防寒、防暑、防雨、防风。

3.新疆景色奇丽壮美，与众不同，景点繁多。每次出游，尽可能多带一些电池、胶卷与像带，数码相机要带上充电器，如果内存不够，最好带数码伴侣。

4.新疆少数民族众多，风情风俗各异，注意尊重少数民族风俗习惯。

图书在版编目(CIP)数据

快乐中国——学汉语：新疆篇·下/《快乐中国——学汉语》栏目组编．—北京：北京语言大学出版社，2006
ISBN 978-7-5619-1659-9

Ⅰ．快…　Ⅱ．快…　Ⅲ．汉语－视听教学－对外汉语教学－教材　Ⅳ．H195.4

中国版本图书馆CIP数据核字（2006）第062947号

书　　名：快乐中国——学汉语：新疆篇·下
中文编辑：于　晶　　　　整体设计：张志伟
英文编辑：侯晓娟　　　　责任印制：汪学发
部分图片提供：徐　俊

出版发行：北京语言大学出版社
社　　址：北京市海淀区学院路15号　　邮政编码：100083
网　　址：www.blcup.com
电　　话：发行部　82303648/3591/3651
编辑部　82303647
读者服务部　82303653/3908
网上订购电话　82303668
客户服务信箱　service@blcup.net
印　　刷：北京联兴盛业印刷股份有限公司
经　　销：全国新华书店

版　　次：2011年3月第1版　2011年3月第1次印刷
开　　本：710毫米×980毫米　1/16　印张：13.25
字　　数：173千字
书　　号：ISBN 978-7-5619-1659-9/H·06107
定　　价：78.00元

凡有印装质量问题，本社出版部负责调换。电话：82303590
Printed in China